MASTER GUID

GENERAL EDIT

JANE AUSTEN	*Emma* Norman Page
	Sense and Sensibility Judy Simons
	Persuasion Judy Simons
	Pride and Prejudice Raymond Wilson
	Mansfield Park Richard Wirdnam
SAMUEL BECKETT	*Waiting for Godot* Jennifer Birkett
WILLIAM BLAKE	*Songs of Innocence and Songs of Experience* Alan Tomlinson
ROBERT BOLT	*A Man for All Seasons* Leonard Smith
CHARLOTTE BRONTË	*Jane Eyre* Robert Miles
EMILY BRONTË	*Wuthering Heights* Hilda D. Spear
JOHN BUNYAN	*The Pilgrim's Progress* Beatrice Batson
GEOFFREY CHAUCER	*The Miller's Tale* Michael Alexander
	The Pardoner's Tale Geoffrey Lester
	The Wife of Bath's Tale Nicholas Marsh
	The Knight's Tale Anne Samson
	The Prologue to the Canterbury Tales Nigel Thomas and Richard Swan
JOSEPH CONRAD	*The Secret Agent* Andrew Mayne
CHARLES DICKENS	*Bleak House* Dennis Butts
	Great Expectations Dennis Butts
	Hard Times Norman Page
GEORGE ELIOT	*Middlemarch* Graham Handley
	Silas Marner Graham Handley
	The Mill on the Floss Helen Wheeler
T. S. ELIOT	*Murder in the Cathedral* Paul Lapworth
	Selected Poems Andrew Swarbrick
HENRY FIELDING	*Joseph Andrews* Trevor Johnson
E. M. FORSTER	*A Passage to India* Hilda D. Spear
	Howards End Ian Milligan
WILLIAM GOLDING	*The Spire* Rosemary Sumner
	Lord of the Flies Raymond Wilson
OLIVER GOLDSMITH	*She Stoops to Conquer* Paul Ranger
THOMAS HARDY	*The Mayor of Casterbridge* Ray Evans
	Tess of the d'Urbervilles James Gibson
	Far from the Madding Crowd Colin Temblett-Wood
BEN JONSON	*Volpone* Michael Stout
JOHN KEATS	*Selected Poems* John Garrett
RUDYARD KIPLING	*Kim* Leonée Ormond
PHILIP LARKIN	*The Less Deceived* and *The Whitsun Weddings* Andrew Swarbrick

MACMILLAN MASTER GUIDES

DOCTOR FAUSTUS

BY CHRISTOPHER MARLOWE

DAVID A. MALE

MACMILLAN

First published 1985 by
THE MACMILLAN PRESS LTD
Houndmills, Basingstoke, Hampshire RG21 2XS
and London
Companies and representatives
throughout the world

ISBN 0–333–37939–X

A catalogue record for this book is available
from the British Library.

Printed in Malaysia

10 9   8   7   6   5   4   3
05 04 03 02 01 00 99 98

CONTENTS

GENERAL EDITOR'S PREFACE

The aim of the Macmillan Master Guides is to help you to appreciate the book you are studying by providing information about it and by suggesting ways of reading and thinking about it which will lead to a fuller understanding. The section on the writer's life and background has been designed to illustrate those aspects of the writer's life which have influenced the work, and to place it in its personal and literary context. The summaries and critical commentary are of special importance in that each brief summary of the action is followed by an examination of the significant critical points. The space which might have been given to repetitive explanatory notes has been devoted to a detailed analysis of the kind of passage which might confront you in an examination. Literary criticism is concerned with both the broader aspects of the work being studied and with its detail. The ideas which meet us in reading a great work of literature, and their relevance to us today, are an essential part of our study, and our Guides look at the thought of their subject in some detail. But just as essential is the craft with which the writer has constructed his work of art, and this is considered under several technical headings – characterisation, language, style and stagecraft.

The authors of these Guides are all teachers and writers of wide experience, and they have chosen to write about books they admire and know well in the belief that they can communicate their admiration to you. But you yourself must read and know intimately the book you are studying. No one can do that for you. You should see this book as a lamp-post. Use it to shed light, not to lean against. If you know your text and know what it is saying about life, and how it says it, then you will enjoy it, and there is no better way of passing an examination in literature.

JAMES GIBSON

ACKNOWLEDGEMENTS

Quotations are taken from the Everyman edition of Marlowe's plays:
E. D. Pendry and J. C. Maxwell (eds), *Christopher Marlowe: Complete
Plays and Poems* (London: Dent, 1976).

Cover illustration is an original sketch of *Doctor Faustus* © Philip Rundle.

GENERAL INTRODUCTION

Shakespeare's *A Midsummer Night's Dream* includes a scene in which some workmen, unskilled at acting, rehearse a play. One of them, Flute, a bellows-mender by trade, has been allotted the female role. He is very uncertain as to what is required of him. When he finally appears on the stage during a rehearsal he blurts out all that he has so painfully learnt. But the producer immediately reprimands him with the words: 'You speak all your part at once, cues and all.' Flute had learnt all his words and recited them in one continuous speech. There was nothing in his script to suggest that this was not the right action. His error is easily explained. The Elizabethan actor did not have the whole of the play written out, but only the words of his own speeches with a few lines from the previous speaker as cues to warn him when to begin. Only the producer's copy of the play would contain instructions for entrances and exits.

We must be careful not to fall into a similar trap when we read the text of a play by assuming that the words printed on the page *are* the play. Indeed they are not. We must recognise that the script of a play is very different from the text of a novel or a poem and requires quite different responses from us as readers.

The novelist puts his or her thoughts and ideas together on paper, and after much revision, rewriting and alteration, those revised thoughts are published in the form of a novel or short story. The printed text, representing a tidied-up version of the author's original manuscript, is directly available to the reader. In the case of the playwright, the process is entirely different: the words are not directed to the reader but to an audience through the medium of performance. There is a world of difference between the reader silently absorbed in a novel and that same person in a theatre watching a play. Instead of deciphering the text, the eyes are taking in a whole host of visual impressions; the ears, far from ignoring extraneous noises, are engaged in listening to the sounds of speech and music; and the imagination is responding to what is seen and heard rather than forming impressions from the printed text on the page.

Perhaps the text of a play may best be considered as a printed set of instructions given to a group of performers in the hope that they will be translated into action on the stage in such a way that they still represent the author's original intention. Playwrights depend on these actors as their agents of communication. Sometimes the writer gives very precise instructions as to what the stage picture is to look like, the movements required from the actors and the particular way that lines are to be spoken. At other times no precise information is given and the actors have to guess or deduce what is needed.

Let us look at a short piece of text from Marlowe's *Doctor Faustus* as an illustration of the idea of text as 'instruction'. Faustus has made a trip to Rome in company with Mephostophilis and their intention is to play some tricks on the Pope and his entourage. Faustus has been provided with a magic girdle that allows him to become invisible, and Mephostophilis, as a spirit, can disappear at will. In the banquet scene Faustus and Mephostophilis are visible to the audience but not to the participants in the feast.

POPE: Lord Archbishop of Rheims, sit down with us.
ARCHBISHOP: I thank your holiness.
FAUSTUS: Fall to; the devil choke you an you spare.
POPE: Who's that spoke? Friars, look about.
      Lord Raymond, pray fall to, I am beholding
      To the Bishop of Milan for this so rare a present.
FAUSTUS: I thank you, sir.   *[Snatch it]*
POPE: How now? Who snatch'd the meat from me?
      Villains, why speak you not?
      My good Lord Archbishop, here's a most dainty dish
      Was sent me from a cardinal in France.
FAUSTUS: I'll have that too.   *[Snatch it]*
POPE: What lollards do attend our holiness
      That we receive such great indignity? Fetch me some wine.
FAUSTUS: Ay, pray do, for Faustus is a-dry.
POPE: Lord Raymond. I drink unto your grace.
FAUSTUS: I pledge your grace.   *[Snatch it]*
POPE: My wine gone too? Ye lubbers, look about
      And find the man that doth this villainy,
      Or by our sanctitude you all shall die.
      I pray, my lords, have patience at this troublesome banquet.
                           (III.ii. 57–77)

The banquet has been prepared and the Pope invites the Archbishop of Rheims and Raymond, King of Hungary to sit down with him for the celebration of the Feast of St Peter. All would, no doubt, be splendidly garbed in ecclesiastical or royal vestments appropriate to such a ceremony, completely unaware of the lurking, unseen, grinning Faustus and Mephostophilis. The delicate food, exquisitely prepared, has been received as a gift from bishops and cardinals. The scene is set for a formal, ceremonious occasion. The first shock comes when the Pope graciously invites the Archbishop to sit, and cannot believe his ears as he hears 'Fall to; the devil choke you an you spare'. Could such words have come from the Archbishop? But this is the first of many surprises. As he lifts the meat to his lips, he finds it snatched away. When he offers a dish to the Archbishop this too disappears. The Pope is now seriously disconcerted. Calling for wine, he attempts a toast to Raymond, King of Hungary, only to find that the wine has mysteriously evaporated into thin air. The only people that the Pope can find to blame are the waiting friars whom he calls 'villains', 'lollards', 'lubbers'. One can imagine their astonishment, which soon turns to fear as the Pope angrily demands that they find the culprit or suffer death.

Within a few lines, Marlowe has changed a moment of solemn feasting into hilarious comedy. Food and drink fly through the air. Tempers become frayed. Angry accusations are hurled at the friars. The Pope tries to urge patience but the upset continues when a few lines later he receives 'a box on the ears'.

Clearly the scene derives its amusement, not from the wittiness of the words, but the carefully orchestrated action on stage. Whilst we know that the meat and the wine is snatched, the particular responses of the actors playing the Pope, Archbishop and King will have to be invented. The words suggest a sense of growing indignation which the actors must reveal in performance. The stage picture is that of a sumptuous banquet with the Pope in the place of honour, flanked by his distinguished guests and with serving friars anxious that the proceedings will run smoothly. In this formal arrangement, Faustus and Mephostophilis dart about causing upset and dismay. In terms of acting, arranging the setting, organising the disappearing food and wine, the scene demands very careful attention and planning. No specific responses are given to the Archbishop or the King, yet they must contribute to the feeling of general annoyance and growing desperation. Perhaps as dutiful guests they are reluctant to admit that anything is amiss, but they are soon drawn into the action. The waiting friars are given no words to speak but they are subject to strong abuse to which they must respond. Will they reveal the injustice of the accusations or submit to the remonstrances? In about twenty lines of dialogue, Marlowe has created a complex, highly amusing, visually attractive sequence where the joy lies in what is seen rather than heard. The words, however, provide the shape and the evidence from which the action and the characterisation will be developed.

The reader sitting at home may occasionally laugh or smile at an amusing passage as a private response to what he or she finds funny. In the theatre, as the above example illustrates, the vigour of the stage action will provoke a much greater response from the audience. The performers, sensing these reactions, may adjust some element of the presentation as a consequence. Actors will often talk of a play 'going well tonight' when reactions are quick and sensitive or of a 'sticky audience' which seems slow to respond to the play. Members of the audience, far from being passive, show approval or disapproval through applause or booing, perhaps even abruptly leaving the theatre in boredom, annoyance or anger. Not until the words of the playwright have reached that audience can the text, as drama, be said to have any real existence.

We can now begin to see what an immense burden the text of a play carries with all the information it must contain and the deductions and implications that are drawn from it. Except for stage instructions, the text is written entirely in direct speech, to be spoken by individual characters. Not only must attention be paid to the sound and pattern of the vocalised words, but they must be appropriate to the character speaking them, indicating, suggesting, implying his or her particular personality, attitude or mood. The literary style in which a play is written may vary from grand, flowing poetic language to words that seem very ordinary, every-day, colloquial. We shall find Marlowe using a variety of styles within a single play. But whatever the style it must be vocally vivid, capable of creating credible characters, and rich in information about the setting or environment of the play.

The whole of the plot and the development of the drama must also be contained in the dialogue and the actions it suggests. The playwright will, therefore, carefully select events and places in the story that allow the plot to be revealed most effectively. It is very rare for a play, unlike a novel, to tell the whole story. We usually find a selection of episodes that are particularly important and significant forming the substance of the play, whilst the rest of the narrative is carefully filled out through odd remarks, recollections or sometimes, as is the case with *Doctor Faustus*, by using a narrator.

In summary we may say that the words of the dramatic text have the following functions:

1. They create the literary or poetic style of the play.
2. They provide details from which characterisation can be developed.
3. They carry the plot of the play and its dramatic structure through a series of episodes animated by language in action.
4. They suggest the environment of the action and evoke particular moods or feelings.

When the text moves into actual production, the demands are further extended so that the words also:

5. provide ideas for staging the play;
6. offer suggestions to designers for settings and costumes.

Those words that look so inanimate on the page, when spoken may induce hushed silence or provoke hearty laughter. This strange power is derived partly from the meaning and emotion that the words contain, but also from their sound, the accents in which they are spoken, the careful use of pauses, the timing of phrases and emphasis. The words, in performance, magically create for us a reality that takes us imaginatively into that strange wood where the Mechanicals rehearse their play or into the portals of the Pope's palace to share the high jinks in which Faustus and Mephostophilis so joyfully indulge. As John Styan writes in *The Dramatic Experience* (Cambridge University Press, 1965, p.53), 'It is not the words alone which make the play, but the vivid dramatic impressions which the words can create.' When reading a play, we must be constantly on the alert, responsive to those impressions that build in our imagination a picture of dramatic reality.

1 CHRISTOPHER MARLOWE: LIFE AND BACKGROUND

1.1 LIFE

Christopher Marlowe was born in 1564, the same year as William Shakespeare, but he was killed in 1593, aged 29, as a result of a brawl in a tavern at Deptford, just outside London. In the mêlée he was stabbed in the eye and the wound proved fatal. This sordid incident, said to have arisen as a result of a quarrel about the settlement of the bill, brought to a premature end the life of a playwright whose brilliance dazzled and excited his Elizabethan audiences. The killing, however, was surrounded by some mystery. We know that two weeks before the Deptford incident a warrant had been issued for Marlowe's arrest and more recent investigations carried out by Leslie Hotson (*The Death of Christopher Marlowe*, 1925) reveal that about a month later Marlowe's assassin, Ingram Frizer, received a Queen's pardon, asserting that the killing had been in self defence. There was no post-mortem or trial. It has been suggested that the murder of Marlowe was a pre-arranged political assassination. For some reason the authorities wanted Marlowe silenced.

He appears to have been a rather dangerous character. A year or so earlier, in 1592, he had been rebuked for disturbing the Queen's peace and before that he had been arrested because of alleged involvement in a murder. Reports claim that he was quick tempered, always ready to pick a quarrel and had frequent brushes with the law. Earlier in his career, a very different picture emerges. We find the Queen's Council commending him for his good services carried out for the benefit of his country. How could a man at one time held in such regard by the Government become a candidate for political murder?

The story is a complex one and in its telling we can observe how much of Marlowe's own restless, inquisitive, provocative personality invades his dramatic characters. The plays are in no sense autobiographical, but they do illustrate the ideas and themes that Marlowe found intriguing. A book about Christopher Marlowe by Harry Levin is entitled *The Overreacher*. This description identifies Marlowe's constant striving, reaching out into new, unexplored territory, challenging orthodox beliefs and values, shocking authority with brisk assertions and denunciations, particularly in matters of religious belief and theological doctrine. The simplest way to trace his complex life is to look at it chronologically.

Born in Canterbury in 1564, the son of a shoemaker, at the age of 15 he gained a scholarship to the King's School, Canterbury. In 1580 he went on to study at Corpus Christi College in Cambridge, having received a scholarship, the gift of Matthew Parker, Archbishop of Canterbury. The holder of such an award was usually expected to become a priest. Although Marlowe held the scholarship for six years, there is no indication that he ever intended to take holy orders. Indeed, we find him mysteriously absent from Cambridge for long periods, much to the annoyance of the University authorities. He seems to have travelled to Rheims in France where there was a college for training English Catholics. Little wonder that the Protestant University officers were annoyed. So much so, that they refused to award him his Master's degree. But at this point the government stepped in. An order from the Privy Council asserted that he had been of good service to the Queen, employed for the benefit of his country and the degree of MA was duly bestowed. It can only be assumed that Marlowe's absences abroad were not concerned with possible conversion to Catholicism, as was suspected, but that he was a secret agent of the Government which was anxious to discover what was happening in Europe. The head of the governmental enquiries was Sir Francis Walsingham whose name will occur again in this history. At a very early age, Marlowe had entered the dangerous world of espionage – just how dangerous he was to discover later.

Spying had not been Marlowe's only occupation. Although not a noted scholar at Cambridge, he had begun to experiment in writing poetry and plays, often producing English verse translations of classical Latin poets. In the year that he left Cambridge, his massive two-part play *Tamburlaine* was produced in a London theatre and was immediately successful. As well as *Doctor Faustus* (date uncertain), Marlowe also wrote *The Jew of Malta* (1590), *Edward II* (1592), and a lesser known play *The Massacre at Paris* (date uncertain). These major plays all illustrate Marlowe's obsession with the 'overreacher' whose individualistic, striving ambitions or personal desires drive him into challenging, dangerous and ultimately tragic actions.

We see that Marlowe's real life was equally challenging and dangerous. His career was littered with arguments, fights, killings and associations with fellow writers and thinkers who were to prove his undoing. Amongst his friends were Sir Walter Raleigh and the playwright Thomas Kyd, members of a group called by some 'The School of Night' who were suspected of both atheism and treason. On 12 May 1593, Kyd was arrested and probably put to torture in order to extract a confession from him. What he did was to denounce his former friend and room-mate, claiming that Marlowe had scoffed at many passages of scripture and made derogatory remarks about Christ, the apostle John and St Paul. He had derided the scriptures, mocked prayer and contradicted much biblical writing and theological scholarship. Such damning evidence, questionable since it was secured under duress, was sufficient to bring a warrant for Marlowe's arrest.

Worse was to come. At the beginning of June 1593 a severe indictment of Marlowe's beliefs was published by one Richard Baines (known to be a government informer). Amongst the allegations (listed in full in J. B. Steane, *Marlowe: A Critical Study*, Appendix 1) were the following:

> That the Indians and many authors of antiquity have assuredly written of above sixteen thousand years ago whereas Adam is proved to have lived within six thousand years.
> He affirms that Moses was but a juggler. . .
> That Christ was a bastard and his mother dishonest.
> That they that love not tobacco and boys were fools.

The testimony concluded with the ominous words 'he persuades men to Atheism. . . utterly scorning both God and his ministers and urges that a mouth of so dangerous a member may be stopped'. So the last eventful and fateful months of Marlowe's life began with the warrant out for his arrest and Baines' condemnatory document. He was a marked man who had clearly become an embarrassment to the Government he had previously served so faithfully and efficiently; better that one with such atheistic, revolutionary tendencies should be silenced. Marlowe's less than innocent companions on the day that he died have been identified from the coroner's inquest. Ingram Frizer, who received the Queen's pardon, was known to be in the pay of Walsingham, the Government spy chief, Nicholas Skeres was probably a Government agent, and Robert Poley was also known to be a spy. A quarrel broke out in which it was alleged that Marlowe attacked Frizer, wounding him with Frizer's own dagger. The slightly injured man managed to snatch back his weapon, lunged at Marlowe, wounding him in the eye. The blow appeared to be fatal. The account fails to explain the roles of the other two men. They did not seem to intercept Marlowe's attack or intervene when Frizer struck back. All we know is that Marlowe died shortly afterwards and that within a month Frizer was cleared of homicide. The life of Marlowe the overreacher, so rich in promise, ended in what looked like political assassination. Marlowe's earlier service to Walsingham did not protect him when his name became associated with atheism and treason. The heroes of Marlowe's plays were all ambitious high fliers. Each died in sudden decline, horror or annihilation.

1.2 OTHER PLAYS

Whilst at Cambridge, Marlowe, as well as translating the poems of Ovid and Lucan, may also having been working on *Dido, Queen of Carthage*. His growing mastery of poetic forms is evidenced in the rich, sensual vigour and variety of the verse. The plot operates on an earthly level and also aloft amongst the immortals. By intermingling the clash of desire and will in god and man, Marlowe creates a unified universe.

The play tells of Aeneas, a Trojan prince, seeking refuge in Italy, who finds himself and his fleet storm-bound on the shores of North Africa. Dido, the widowed Queen of Carthage is emotionally drawn to him and attempts to persuade Aeneas to stay rather than pursue further exploits in Italy. Though there is a strong, almost magnetic attraction between them, Aeneas, prompted by Hermes, messenger of the gods, eventually leaves Carthage. The Queen, discovering herself abandoned, commits suicide. The plot is complicated by the actual appearance of gods and goddesses. They make their presence felt by direct means such as creating storms to prevent sailing, but also in curious impersonations.

Cupid, son of the goddess Venus, disguises himself as the son of Aeneas in order to advance the love affair between Aeneas and Dido. The play actually begins with a scene which depicts sporting and quarrelling amongst the gods and then the action transfers to the coast of Carthage.

Though there is some weakness in the dramatic construction, we can see clearly lively characterisation and deeply emotional feelings which boil over into jealousy, rejection, sorrow and death. A vivid example of the intensity evoked in Marlowe's poetry is found in the episode where Dido awaits the arrival of Aeneas. She declares:

> I'll make me bracelets of his golden hair;
> His glistering eyes shall be my looking glass;
> His lips an altar, where I'll offer up
> As many kisses as the sea hath sands;
> Instead of music I will hear him speak;
> His looks shall be my only library;
> And thou, Aeneas, Dido's treasury,
> In whose fair bosom I will lock more wealth
> Than twenty thousand Indias can afford.   (III. i. 85-93)

She almost blushes at the immodesty of her thoughts. The vibrant, exciting, exotic nature of this verse indicates the form and style that Marlowe's poetry will take.

The two parts of *Tamburlaine* tell the story of a man who through ruthless fanaticism beats a path to world leadership, trampling mercilessly on all who oppose him. Emperors, kings, captains, fall beneath his vanquishing armies. The end of Part I shows him at the zenith of his political and military power and betrothed to an enchantingly beautiful Egyptian princess, Zenocrate. Though the 'bloody conquests' continue in Part II, the upward path becomes less certain. Zenocrate falls ill and dies, Tamburlaine, in a burst of angry irritation, kills his son Calyphas in cold blood. Following a murderous attack on the city of Babylon, Tamburlaine orders all copies of the holy books of Islam, including the Koran, to be burnt. In this irreligious action, the tyrant has gone too far. Suddenly he finds his strength diminishing. Now there are challenges to his authority which he is too weak to resist. All his former glory fades and he dies handing over authority to his surviving son.

We notice the huge canvas of the world that Marlowe paints for his characters to inhabit. Tamburlaine seems like an unstoppable superman.

His relentless ambition, his inhuman cruelty, the bloodshed, violence and suffering that he leaves in his wake do not make him a character we can admire. But we are left breathless by his audacity, the scope and range of his conquests, all of which Marlowe depicts in startling, violent stage action. Kings are contained in cages or made to draw Tamburlaine's chariot. Murders and massacres abound. Wars, sieges, single combats all find their place on the stage as Tamburlaine moves forward on his bloodthirsty conquests. In this play Marlowe shows an amazing ability to shape a complex torrent of diverse events into a drama that traces the rise and fall of the world conqueror.

The scale of *The Jew of Malta* is much smaller than *Tamburlaine* but the same intensity of feeling and directness of response remains. Marlowe uses the figure of Machiavelli, renowned for his treatise on political expediency and cunning, to introduce a play in which Barabas, a rich Jew living in Malta, forced to give up his possessions to the authorities is quick to plan cunning and vicious revenges. The tribute demanded is to pay off the Turkish overlords. Barabas has hidden part of his wealth under the floorboards, but his house has been taken by the authorities as part of the sequestration of his possessions. His daughter, Abigail, goes to the house, now converted to a nunnery, alleging her desire to join the order. She gains access and manages to recover the Jew's rich possessions. Now Barabas determines to revenge himself on the Christians and employs a villainous Arab, Ithamore, in his plans. Lodowick, the Governor's son, and a young gentleman named Matthias are the first victims. Both are in love with Abigail, and Barabas unscrupulously uses his daughter as a decoy. Dismayed by this discovery and the deaths of the young men, Abigail decides to go to the nunnery in earnest. An angry Barabas sends poisoned food there and all including Abigail die. But she has denounced her father as the assassin of Lodowick and Matthias. In an attempt to avoid condemnation, Barabas pretends to convert to Christianity, but, in turn, he is betrayed by Ithamore. At first he avoids arrest by feigning death and then plots and counterplots with Turks and Christians. A plan is proposed to demolish the monastery in which the Turkish troops are stationed but it misfires. Barabas, hoping to trap his enemies, finds himself the victim when he falls into a cauldron of boiling oil that he has placed in readiness to dispose of his opponents.

Marlowe clearly shows his intention in *The Jew of Malta* by using Machiavelli as his Prologue. Popularly interpreted, his political and moral theories advocate, amongst other things, the importance of might against right and the value of deceit in diplomacy. He declares: 'I count religion but a childish toy,/And hold there is no sin but ignorance' (Prologue 14-15). There is praise for the wily, the deceitful, the cunning, and Barabas is to be the example in this play. There is little to admire in Barabas, but his energy, persistence, heartlessness and subtlety surprise and shock us. There seems to be no villainy or cruelty to which he will not descend if it proves necessary. He uses his daughter and his servant as instruments of his policy and they in turn finally denounce or betray him. This callous indifference to human suffering almost makes Barabas a monster. But he lives in a corrupt society. Politicians, military and religious leaders are all tainted. As a Jew, Barabas is inevitably an outsider, a ready victim for Christian assault. The subject of the play cannot be thought of as that of an evil Jew against a saintly Christian society, but rather as that of a man responding to the spirit of the times, ingeniously using current corrupt practices and deceits to his own purposes. We do not find, as we shall in *Doctor Faustus*, a moral epilogue. The overall scope of the play is narrow, never moving beyond Malta, but there is diversity in the sequence of bloodthirsty events and the ingenuity of the stage action, and the language is rich, exotic and colourful. The excess and subtlety of Barabas's plotting makes him an overreacher. How apt and horrific that he should drown in a pot of boiling oil intended for his adversaries!

We can now see quite clearly from these examples of Tamburlaine and Barabas, the kind of person that intrigues Marlowe the playwright. He is obsessed by the man who challenges, who rejects orthodox restrictions, and is possessed by a wild fearlessness that drives him to excesses, ambition, or revenge. Tamburlaine wants to change the pattern of the world to his own advantage. Barabas, unwilling to accept the unjust sequestration of his goods, seeks horrible revenges. In the play of *Edward II*, the English King finds an unacceptable division between what are regarded as the duties and responsibilities of the monarch and his personal, consuming love for a young courtier, Piers Gaveston. This homosexual relationship is universally condemned by the barons of England, but Edward flouts their opinion and brings Gaveston back from exile and heaps him with honours. Such action rouses the animosity of the nobles to an even higher pitch and they plan to rid the country of this profligate King. Mortimer emerges as the leader of the opposition and embarks on a course that eventually leads him to the throne. Gaveston is murdered, but the King takes another favourite, Spencer. During military skirmishes Mortimer is captured, but he escapes, enlists the aid of Edward's estranged wife Isabella and leads an army against Edward who is forced to abdicate. The King is then imprisoned in Berkeley Castle. An ambiguous message sent by Mortimer secures Edward's murder in horrible and degrading circumstances. In causing the King's death, Mortimer finds himself attacked. He too becomes a victim and is imprisoned and then executed in the Tower of London at the command of Edward's youthful son.

The focus of this play is, of course, different from Marlowe's other tragedies since it develops from the actual history surrounding the reign of Edward II (1284–1327). Marlowe uses the person of an English monarch to create a central figure, dying tragically; defeated by unrestricted desires which do not match up to the role of king. Edward wilfully persists in his personal desires against all remonstrance and suffers in consequence. We should also notice that Mortimer, too, exhibits powerful ambitions which lead him to overstretch himself. He sees himself as a victim of Fortune. Having risen on Fortune's ever turning wheel and reaching the highest point, the only subsequent direction possible is downwards. In the figure of Mortimer, Marlowe presents us with another overreacher. Desire for world supremacy, pursuit of riches, self-gratification, vaulting ambition – these are the remorseless urges that Marlowe's heroes all seem to possess. They are driven into acts of daring, cruelty, danger, revenge and, ultimately, self-destruction. Whatever the scale of the operation, whether over continents and kingdoms or in city states, we find those societies peopled by all the hierarchies and panoplies of authority. Marlowe's plays are nearly always full of kings, emperors, princes, knights, governors, generals, bishops, priests; and the events we witness are always of national or international significance. All the world is Marlowe's stage. His brilliant, grandiose, frightening epics are not only created in the stage spectacle of bloody conquests, gruesome murders, ignominious defeats but in the fertile flow of his poetry – inspiring, unbounded, rich in imagery, humming with verbal resonance and appealing to the ear in its splendour, its marching rhythms. Our imagination is jolted by the revelation of intimate relationships couched in sensuous, exotic verse. This is the kind of writing experience and skill that Marlowe brings to *Doctor Faustus*.

1.3 *DOCTOR FAUSTUS*

All of Marlowe's plays were written in so short a time that it is not always possible to be absolutely precise in identifying the order of their production. But it is generally agreed that *Doctor Faustus* is Marlowe's final play. The actual text, however, is surrounded by almost as many mysteries as Marlowe's death. Academic argument continues to flourish as to which of two texts, one published in 1604 and the second in 1616, more precisely represents the play that Marlowe actually wrote. Theatre records show that *Doctor Faustus* was performed on many occasions before 1604, but no texts of those performances seem to exist. The first published version is called the A text and the 1616 edition is called the B text. Considerable variations exist between the two texts. A is much shorter and naturally includes fewer episodes than the second version. (A very full comparison of the two texts will be found in the edition prepared by W. W. Greg (ed.), *Marlowe's Dr. Faustus 1604–1616: Parallel Texts*.) Evidence suggests that other authors might have been involved in writing the play. We know that in 1602 (before the publication of the A text) William Bird and Samuel Rowley were paid a substantial fee for their additions to the extant version. The name of John Nashe has also been suggested as a collaborator. He was a member, along with Marlowe, of a group of young poets and playwrights known as the University Wits. With suspected traces of all these authors' writing in the play, establishing authorship is tricky. For a number of years, preference was expressed for the 1616 version, but now this has switched to the shorter text as being more authentically Marlowe's work. It is the sense and texture of the verse in the middle section of the play that gives rise to most argument. Perhaps Marlowe planned the overall structure and collaborators supplied additional material. Group playwriting was quite common in the Elizabethan period. Many plays had more than one author. One version might have been that used by a smaller travelling company with fewer actors in the group, whilst the longer version was presented when the Company were at their London base. The conjecture, though academically intriguing, is not particularly helpful to a student meeting the text for the first time. All modern editions of the play use the 1616 version with notes of its relationship to the earlier publication. The comments in this book relate to the longer text, with indications where there is some doubt or argument about the authorship.

There can be little doubt about the main source of inspiration to Marlowe for his play of *Doctor Faustus*. We have already discovered his particular interest in a central character always eager to extend his own horizons, break conventions, employing dangerous, even cruel methods if necessary to fulfil his ambitions. Though both Tamburlaine and Edward II had a real historical existence, Marlowe did not attempt a true dramatic reconstruction of their lives, but selected or invented events that allow the central character to express his personal dramatic intention, preferably on a grand scale. It so happened that an almost perfect subject was presented to him. There appeared in 1592 an English translation of a German book with the title *The Historie of the damnable life and deserved death of Doctor John Faustus*. We only know the initials of the translator - P.F., *Gent*. The English *Faustbook* was not a play, but a collection of essays, anecdotes and reports about a German scholar named Faustus who dabbled in magic. He appears to have been something of a ne'er-do-well, but he gained a reputation for his necromantic skills. Stories, no doubt exaggerated, abounded about his activities. But this traffic in magic and witchcraft brought the German doctor to a horrific end - not surprising since his actions were totally irreligious and condemned by the Church as dealing with the Devil. The account ends with the story of a howling wind that battered the house where Faustus lay on his deathbed. Students, also in the house, heard 'a mighty noise and hissing, as if the hall had been full of snakes and adders'. Screams for help were heard and the next morning the students found the room 'besprinkled with blood and his (Faustus's) brains cleaving to the wall'. The mangled body was found lying in a pile of horse manure in the yard outside. It is clear from this brief reference to the death of the German Doctor Faustus that Marlowe did not simply dramatise the text as he found it, but used the eminently suitable material to shape his own *Tragical History of the Life and Death of Doctor Faustus*. Here was an overreacher *par excellence*: a learned scholar breaking the bounds of religious restrictions, achieving power, notoriety and admiration, and suffering a terrible death because of his apostasy. Perhaps the author transfers some of his own revolutionary feelings to the character he creates in *Doctor Faustus*. We might expect, though, that Marlowe would cause his protagonist to escape retribution, knowing of the writer's reported contempt for the emptiness or shallowness of religious faith. However the title of Marlowe's play differs significantly from the German Faust Book. A 'damnable life and deserved death' becomes a 'tragical history'. Marlowe the playwright maintains a *tragic* structure as he has done in all his other plays. Though the characters may represent the outpouring of his own unorthodox, revolutionary thoughts, in no case does their ambition, desire or greed avoid retribution. Marlowe stays loyal to his classical models. The great Greek tragedies traced the fall of such royal figures as Agamemnon and Oedipus. Triumph was only a prelude to disaster. Shakespeare's *Richard II, Macbeth* and *King Lear* will provide magnificent successors to this concept of tragedy.

There is an irony that Marlowe, apparently so disdainful of religion produces totally orthodox reasons for Faustus's condemnation. We shall discover that imploring figures like the Good Angel and the Old Man repeat only what is theologically sound. Even the evil characters like Lucifer, Mephostophilis, and Belzebub are depicted as fallen angels, ejected from Heaven by virtue of their presumption. The whole universe that Marlowe creates in *Doctor Faustus* is essentially and inescapably Christian. But within that religious framework and classic tragic structure is a compelling drama of a man whose mounting ambition inevitably brings about his 'hellish fall' as he stubbornly rejects repeated advice that his actions must lead to damnation.

2 SUMMARIES
AND
CRITICAL COMMENTARY

Prologue

Summary

The Chorus introduces the chief character of the play, Doctor John Faustus who, although born of peasant stock, has achieved eminence as a brilliant academic in the University of Wittenburg. The speaker gives a brief summary of the main theme, telling how Faustus dabbles in black magic which results in his final damnation. The Chorus concludes with a lament for Faustus's preference for these 'devilish exercises'.

Commentary

The Prologue, with two other Choruses and an Epilogue, mark the stages of Faustus's progress towards damnation with added moralistic comment. The fact that we are told of Faustus's death and damnation removes surprise but provides the basis for a continuous irony.

Act I, Scene i

Summary

Faustus is discovered sitting in his study considering the principal academic disciplines. One by one they are rejected. First he casts aside the study of the great Greek philosopher, Aristotle. Skilful argument is insufficiently rewarded. Medicine is dismissed because it has found no cure for death. Next Divinity is rejected because of the apparent harshness of God's judgement. He chooses to follow black magic, or necromancy, which he believes will bring him immense worldly power and riches. Valdes and Cornelius, two black magicians, are invited to visit Faustus. This decision precipitates the appearance of two figures, the Good Angel representing Faustus's conscience and the Bad Angel who encourages his baser instincts. The Good Angel pleads with Faustus to reconsider his decision while the Bad Angel urges him towards black magic. However Faustus is determined to pursue his aim. His mind is full of riches and political power. Encouraged by his evil visitor, his dreams become extravagant and exotic, embracing the known world and ancient civilisations. He is so glutted with such exciting prospects that Faustus determines to conjure the Devil by following the instructions of his evil counsellors.

Commentary

In this scene the intelligent, learned Faustus makes a fatally unwise decision. Ignoring the advice of his conscience, he makes a deliberate choice to adopt black magic as his chief study. In rejecting Divinity, Faustus failed to complete the quotations which he uttered: 'The reward of sin is death' concludes with 'but the gift of God is eternal life through Jesus Christ our Lord' (Romans, v.i.23). The second verse about sin and self deception should continue with 'If we confess our sins he is faithful and just to forgive us our sins and to cleanse us from all unrighteousness' (I John, 1.8). Faustus emphasises the harshness of judgement and neglects forgiveness and redemption. This is to prove a fatal misreading, surprising for a scholar so versed in the scriptures.

The figures of the Good and Bad Angels are drawn from medieval morality plays. We shall see their constant reappearance in the play whenever Faustus is wavering in his decisions. The Good Angel is a constant reminder of the possibility of repentance and salvation. The Bad Angel is the agent of Satan seducing Faustus into evil by visions of richness and power.

Act I, Scene ii

Summary

In response to an enquiry from two students as to the whereabouts of Doctor Faustus, his servant, Wagner, gives a long-winded reply couched in pseudo-academic argument. Eventually, he reveals that his master is dining with the infamous necromancers, Valdes and Cornelius. The scholars are immediately alarmed at contact with a 'damned art' which puts the soul in jeopardy.

Commentary

The quick-witted servant Wagner introduces a comic element into the
play. He is full of academic jargon, presumably picked up from his
master, and he successfully outsmarts the two scholars in argument.
However, the hazardous nature of the course which Faustus is pursuing
is made very apparent from the outset by the alarm expressed by the
scholars.

Act I, Scene iii

Summary

To the accompaniment of thunder and with Lucifer and his devilish
attendants observing his actions, Faustus begins the process of conjuration. He draws a circle round himself, inscribing on the circumference the Hebrew letters spelling Jehovah, names of saints and signs
of the Zodiac. His invocation in Latin calls on Lucifer, prince of the
east, Belzebub, monarch of burning Hell, and Demogorgon (the devilish
trio equivalent to the heavenly Trinity of God: the Father, Son and
Holy Ghost) to send forth Mephostophilis. At first there is no response,
so he scatters holy water and makes the sign of the cross. Mephostophilis
appears, but in the shape of an ugly dragon. Faustus orders him to
return and reappear in the disguise of a Franciscan friar. Faustus,
exulting in his necromantic skill, proclaims himself 'conjuror laureate'
when Mephostophilis comes back dressed in a friar's habit. The Doctor
quickly discovers that his new-found servant will perform only what
Lucifer allows and that Mephostophilis responded to his conjuration
not as an order, but as an opportunity to secure another candidate for
Hell. Faustus makes light of these references to Hell, believing them to
be inventions of the philosophers. Nor is he terrified by threats of
damnation. Mephostophilis describes Lucifer, Prince of Hell, as once
beloved by God, but cast out of Heaven because of an attempted
usurpation of God's throne. Angels who joined the conspiracy with
Lucifer were also damned and expelled to Hell. A disbelieving Faustus
receives a powerful remonstrance from Mephostophilis who, having
personal experience of the ecstasy of Heaven and the deprivations of
Hell, urges him to cease these necromantic practices. Faustus remains
unmoved by this surprisingly passionate outburst. Instead he proposes
a treaty with Lucifer that, in exchange for twenty-four years of volup-

tuous living and earthly pre-eminence, he will surrender his soul to the Devil. Left alone, Faustus considers great schemes of domination.

Commentary
This is one of the most important scenes in the play. It firmly establishes Faustus's determination to employ his necromantic power, and it introduces the vital contract with Lucifer. But it also reveals the complex character of Mephostophilis. His desire to catch the soul of Faustus is set against a passionate warning against frivolity. Faustus, deaf to that warning, seems unable to recognise the restrictions that limit his apparent power. Despite Mephostophilis's graphic description of Heaven and Hell, Faustus remains adamant in proposing a bargain with Lucifer that clearly risks damnation. Though Faustus thinks he is in control of the situation, it is apparent that Mephostophilis and Lucifer, who has overlooked the whole proceedings, are a much greater force than Faustus imagines. Despite his alleged wisdom, Faustus falls easily into the clutches of the Devil, even though he has been warned of the dangers by one who offered personal testimony.

Act I, Scene iv

Summary
Wagner has picked up some of his master's conjuring skills which he shows off to a rather foolish, down-at-heel lackey named Robin whom he wishes to employ. Robin is alternately offered bribes and threats. When he rejects the money, Wagner successfully conjures up two devils who attack the frightened lad. Cowed into submission, he receives an assurance that he too will learn these conjuring tricks.

Commentary
This is the first of a series of comic episodes which offer a contrast to and parody of the main events of the play. Wagner, unlike his master, effortlessly conjures up devils without risk to his soul. The devils appear at his bidding and obey his instructions unquestioningly.

Act II, Scene i

Summary
The exultation that Faustus experienced is now replaced by grave uncertainty. Thoughts turning him to God and Heaven battle with a resolution to maintain trust in Belzebub. This inward turmoil is out-

wardly demonstrated by the appearance of two figures: the Bad Angel who urges him to continue his allegiance to Lucifer, and the Good Angel who commends repentance. Having offered these contradictory pieces of advice, the angels vanish. Faustus, consoling himself with visions of wealth, summons up Mephostophilis to hear the outcome of his proposal to Lucifer. He learns that the promise must be enshrined in a formal deed written in blood. Although he remains curious as to the value of his soul to Lucifer, Faustus stabs his arm to obtain the bloody ink. However, to his surprise and puzzlement, the supply dries up and Mephostophilis is despatched to bring fire to revive the flow. Having been warmed, the blood liquefies and the deed is completed with 'Consumatum est' ('It is finished'). At the place of the wound, disturbing words appear: 'Homo fuge' (Flee, O Man), but Faustus determines to resist this advice and stay with Mephostophilis. To quell the evident disturbance in the mind of Faustus, Mephostophilis conjures up devils who make presents of a headdress and rich garments. Thus diverted, the conditions are read over and the signed document delivered. Faustus is eager to ask questions, but he scornfully rejects Mephostophilis's description of the universality of Hell - everywhere except Heaven - and dismisses damnation as an old wives' tale. Soon Faustus discovers limitations to his newly acquired power, so dearly bought. His request for a wife is refused. Instead he is offered a devil dressed as a woman or any courtesan he wishes, as well as a series of books on conjuring, the planets and botany. These gifts seem to content him.

Commentary

The scene identifies the first of a series of moments when Faustus has doubts about his decision. Part of his mind or conscience clings to thoughts of God whilst the rest stays with the Devil. This conflict is personified by the two angels. Whenever that doubt erupts we will notice their appearance. Faustus agrees the contract with the Devil despite two distinct warnings - the drying up of his blood and the message on his arm. He seems strangely shortsighted in rejecting as frivolous Mephostophilis's description of Hell and damnation which the fallen angel has gained from personal experience. In place of a wife he is offered a courtesan and is easily diverted by gifts of books, rather like sweets given to a child.

Faustus has now committed his soul, but the battle for it continues. Time and time again we will observe an increasingly desperate desire for repentance that is always swamped by Lucifer's diversionary tactics.

Act II, Scene ii

Summary

Faustus's conscience again troubles him. Consequently the Good and Bad Angels appear to give their contradictory advice. Faustus tries to dampen his despair with thoughts of pleasure. Much of the information supplied by Mephostophilis is already known. When a question about Heaven arises, an answer is refused. Sensing his unease, the Angels again appear to Faustus, but this last incident prompts the intervention of Lucifer and Belzebub in person, accompanied by Mephostophilis. After a sharp reprimand, they succeed in diverting Faustus's attention with the Show of the Seven Deadly Sins: Pride, Covetousness, Envy, Wrath, Gluttony, Sloth and Lechery. This spectacle has the desired effect and a delighted Faustus is presented with further magic books.

Commentary

This scene develops a recurring pattern; a troubled conscience provokes the appearance of the angels, followed by entertainment to deflect Faustus's mind away from thoughts of repentance. For the first time Lucifer himself participates in the action, which illustrates the seriousness of possible defection on the part of Faustus. The Show of the Seven Deadly Sins is the first of a number of spectacles that we shall see in the play.

Act II, Scene iii

Summary

In this scene, Robin, who has stolen one of Faustus's books, shows off his conjuring abilities to Dick, the ostler. His halting invocation imitates Faustus's words. His chief boast is of a magic power that will provide wine at the local hostelry without payment.

Commentary

This scene offers a comic version of the serious episode of Faustus's conjuration.

Chorus 1

Summary
The Chorus reports on Faustus's careful study of astronomy, his triumphant journeys through the heavens and his determination to visit Rome.

Commentary
By the interjection of this chorus, the action is quickly moved from Germany to Rome. So far Faustus's magic actions have been described rather than demonstrated. In fact, the only necromancy we have seen him perform is the conjuration of Mephostophilis.

Act III, Scene i

Summary
Faustus describes to Mephostophilis his journey through Europe and together they plan to cause mischief in Rome on the occasion of the Pope's celebration of St Peter's Feast. A great procession arrives headed by cardinals and bishops, accompanied by chanting monks and friars. With the Pope is Raymond, King of Hungary, followed by the chained captive Bruno (a rival Pope elected by the German Emperor). The prisoner is used as a footstool for the Pope to ascend his throne. Consideration is given as to the proper punishment for Bruno and two cardinals are despatched to study certain legal documents. Mephostophilis follows the departing clerics and puts them to sleep. He and Faustus assume their robes and return to the council chamber. In the meantime Bruno has unsuccessfully pleaded his cause. Having read out the decree that condemns Bruno to death at the stake, the disguised Faustus and Mephostophilis are made guardians of the prisoner and are able to secure his release. Preparations for the feast then begin.

Commentary
The release of Bruno is probably the last serious act that we see Faustus perform. What follows is a series of comic episodes in which Faustus's actions are hardly distinguishable from those of his servants. The pomp and ceremony surrounding the Pope and his ally, King Raymond, is soon to be thrown into complete disarray.

Act III, Scene ii

Summary

Faustus and Mephostophilis prepare to enjoy the discomfort they will create. Faustus is given a magic belt that renders him invisible. The two unfortunate cardinals, at last returned with their decision about Bruno, find themselves condemned to death by an exasperated Pope. The banquet begins, only to be disturbed by wildly disconcerting events that include the snatching of food and wine by the gleefully invisible Faustus and Mephostophilis. Finally the Pope, getting a box on the ears, orders a group of friars to lay these troublesome ghosts, but the clerics find themselves beaten and chased out with fireworks.

Commentary

This slapstick scene of schoolboy practical jokes is Marlowe's most daring comedy. He pokes fun at the Pope, whose holy person is subject to tricks and physical abuse. The ceremonial of Rome is shattered, the formal dirge accompanied by bell, book and candle descends to an undignified rout with Faustus and Mephosotophilis in comic triumph. Critics have expressed some doubt as to whether Marlowe was the author of these scenes set in Rome. Certainly they are very different in style from other parts of the play. However, the episode could be regarded as an ironic comment on the character of Faustus, making increasingly frivolous use of his dearly bought power. Theatrically speaking, the knockabout comedy would give a special delight to the less educated elements of the audience, whilst the more learned would enjoy the mockery of the Roman Catholic Church rites.

Act III, Scene iii

Summary

Robin and Dick play jokes on a Vintner concerning an alleged stolen wine goblet. They call Mephostophilis to their aid, but he, irritated by this interruption to his duties, transforms Dick into an ape and Robin into a dog.

Commentary

The mob of servants, like Faustus, are equally lighthearted in their conjurations, but they get very short shrift from Mephostophilis when he is commanded to attend them.

Chorus 2

Summary
The Chorus describes the adulation that Faustus receives as he travels back to Germany.

Commentary
This Chorus, whilst reporting the extended debates on astrology, principally serves as an introduction to the scenes in Germany when Faustus demonstrates his magic powers before the Emperor's Court.

Act IV, Scene i

Summary
One courtier, Benvolio, unimpressed by Faustus's powers, is reluctant to join the general admiration extended by Charles, the German Emperor, Bruno and the Duke of Saxony. They welcome Faustus with great effusiveness and he is invited to recreate the historic figures of Alexander the Great and his paramour. Benvolio leaves, making jokes about the venture. The assembled court then watch a dumb show in which Alexander wrestles with and defeats Darius, and presents the crown of the vanquished king to his paramour. The Emperor is so impressed that he moves to embrace the figures, but Faustus warns him 'these are but shadows' and cannot be touched. However, a mole visible on the paramour's neck is proof of her identity. As a punishment for his flippancy, the returning Benvolio finds his head sprouting two horns. Only the kindly intervention of the Emperor prevents him from becoming a permanent figure of fun.

Commentary
Whilst the magic show undoubtedly delighted the German Court, the theatre audience would also enjoy the spectacular conjuration. We are aware, however, of a lack of serious purpose in these scenes which serve to illustrate the trivial use to which Faustus is putting his necromantic skills. Benvolio, who mocks the proceedings, soon feels the sting of the Doctor's irritation. We should also notice that the figures in the Spectacle are untouchable. In a later scene, Faustus will actually embrace the spirit of Helen with dire consequences.

Act IV, Scene ii

Benvolio, annoyed at being made to look foolish, determines to get his
revenge on Faustus. He plans with a group of soldiers to ambush
Faustus. In the ensuing struggle, they believe they have executed him,
but the head they struck off is false and Faustus remains unharmed.
The would-be assassins are chased away by Mephostophilis and other
devils.

Act IV, Scene iii

Summary
This scene is really a continuation of the previous one. Benvolio and his
comrades appear smeared with blood and dirt and all wearing horns –
much to the amusement of the Court.

Commentary
Faustus now seems totally absorbed in rough magic played on an
irritating character of minor importance. Thoughts of grandiose, significant action on a world scale have now completely receded. Faustus
has demonstrated his ability to escape physical harm with comparative
ease, but this will contrast strongly with his failure to escape, however
desperately desired, his final damnation.

Act IV, Scene iv

The next trick is with a horse-dealer, anxious to buy Faustus's mount. A
deal is agreed with the proviso that the horse must never be taken through
water. In a brief soliloquy, after which he sleeps, Faustus is sharply
reminded of his own mortality. The horse-dealer returns. Having
suspected that the proviso was a trick, he foolishly ignored it and his
new purchase disappeared in the water. He attacks Faustus, only to find
the leg he heaves at comes away in his hand. The dealer runs off. Though
disconcerted, he believes he cannot easily be pursued by a one-legged
follower. The torn-off leg is, of course, false and Faustus jokes about
the trick that he has played.

Act IV, Scene v

Summary
Tales of Faustus's magic are now widespread and a carter tells of the consumption of a whole load of hay, whilst the horse-dealer reports his unfortunate experiences. They determine to seek recompense for their losses.

Commentary
Except for the short soliloquy, important because it reminds us of the serious background to these events, the comic style of the play continues in these two scenes. Faustus's magic tricks are little better than schoolboy japes.

Act IV, Scene vi

Summary
Faustus is now the guest of the Duke and Duchess of Vanholt. The lady is presented, at her request, with a dish of out-of-season grapes. The session is interrupted by the arrival of the servants demanding restitution, but Faustus settles them all by a series of magic strokes that render them all dumb.

Commentary
This episode ends the sequence of comic scenes in which Faustus does little more than demonstrate amusing conjuring tricks. It is likely that this section giving such a different character to Faustus was not written by Marlowe but by another author, possibly William Rowley.

Act v, Scene i

Summary
Faustus senses that the end of his life is near. A discourse with his scholars concerning who was the most beautiful woman in the world results in the conjuration of Helen of Troy, whom they all admire. As the scholars depart, an old man appears urging Faustus to give up his devilish necromantic pursuits and turn his mind towards repentance. But this urgent appeal produces in Faustus only deep despair. The feeling is so terrible that Faustus seems willing to accept from Mephostophilis a dagger in order to commit suicide. Although the old man reappears,

stressing the power of God's mercy, Faustus cannot shake off his feelings of hopelessness. He is reprimanded by Mephostophilis for even thinking about repentance. To assuage these desperate thoughts, Faustus re-conjures 'that heavenly Helen'. This time Faustus embraces the spirit and feels his soul drawn from his body. The old man who witnessed the embrace realises that all is lost and now Faustus is indeed damned. The devils are unable to harm the old man, who is also at the end of his life.

Commentary

The most important event in the scene is the conjuration of Helen. Faustus delights in her embrace little realising her devilish power. Immortality, however, is not secured through sensual delight. Instead Faustus ensures his everlasting damnation. This the old man recognises after his unsuccessful attempts to persuade Faustus to repent. We notice once again that a movement towards repentance has been deflected by a show of magic obligingly supplied by Mephostophilis. The devils cannot harm the repentant old man but they are waiting for Faustus.

Act v, Scene ii

Summary

As Faustus engages in settling his earthly affairs, the hordes of Hell assemble to gather up their victim. Nothing that the scholars can say is able to move Faustus from his fixed belief that he is beyond pardon. He then reveals the details of his secret contract with the Devil. Mephostophilis describes how he deliberately misled Faustus with regard to the biblical passages. The entry of the Good and Bad Angels confirm that the time for repentance is past. The Good Angel speaks of the futility of worldly possessions and the Bad Angel enlarges on the horrors of Hell. As the clock strikes eleven, Faustus recognises that his last hour has come.Whatever his wish, the time cannot be slowed down. He sees Christ's redeeming blood streaming in the sky, but a painful rebuke from Lucifer reminds him of his lost state. There is no escape from God's wrath on earth or in the sky, or in his body's dissolution. He faces perpetual damnation. As midnight strikes the devils drag him down into Hell.

Commentary

This scene depicts the profound horror of Faustus's last moments, vividly contrasting the sense of frivolity of the preceding scenes. The episode illustrates the inescapability of God's judgement and the futility of attempts to escape. Christ's blood, the symbol of God's mercy, is clearly apparent to Faustus, but despair prevents genuine repentance and therefore access to that mercy. Faustus suffers the consequences of his pursuit of necromancy. In signing the contract with Lucifer he rejected advice both from the Good Angel and the old man. Power which he has used so foolishly has been bought at the price of his own damnation.

Act v, Scene iii

Summary
The savaged mortal remains of Faustus are discovered by the scholars and taken away for decent burial.

Epilogue

Summary
The Chorus reminds the audience of the dangers associated with the pursuit of practices forbidden by God. The temptation is particularly great for those who consider themselves wise.

Commentary
The final scene and the epilogue are very similar in style to the formal conclusion of a late medieval morality play. The unrepentant sinner is punished and the audience reminded that earthly knowledge does not offer a barrier from the seduction of the Devil. On the contrary, it may be a dangerous inducement to undertake projects that can only end in damnation. The warning through Faustus's example is inescapably plain.

3 THEMES AND ISSUES

Marlowe was writing at a time when there was fierce antagonism towards Roman Catholicism following the break with Rome brought about by Henry VIII and the persecution of Protestants during the reign of Mary Tudor (1553-8). An anti-Catholic play would therefore have been popular. His audience would, for the most part, have strong religious beliefs, be fully aware of the threat of damnation and retain a lively fear of Hell and devils. In stressing Faustus's alliance with Lucifer and thereby ensuring his eternal damnation, Marlowe was making his play conform to current orthodox theology. But this interpretation is very much at odds with the heretical and blasphemous views ascribed to Marlowe. He may have felt constrained by the religious attitude of the time, but perhaps we may detect Marlowe's scepticism in his ability to retain our sympathy for Faustus despite his damnable alliance. It is best perhaps to look at the issues and themes separately before trying to draw any general, overall conclusion.

3.1 RELIGIOUS ELEMENTS

Ironically a very obvious religious tone is given to the play by the presence of a number of devilish characters who are physically represented in the play. The figure of Satan, or Lucifer (the name Marlowe gives him in the play), was God's lieutenant in Heaven until his desire for greater power led to his attempted usurpation of God's throne. As we are reminded in the play, for this presumption he was ejected from Heaven together with other angels who were part of the conspiracy against God.

FAUSTUS: And what are you that live with Lucifer?
MEPHOSTOPHILIS: Unhappy spirits that fell with Lucifer,
    Conspir'd against our God with Lucifer,
    And are for ever damn'd with Lucifer. (I.iv. 69-72)

Now lodged in Hell, this devilish, as opposed to heavenly, trinity consists of Lucifer, Belzebub (both of whom appear in the play) and Demogorgon. Mephostophilis is also a fallen angel, notable for his powerful and affecting speech to Faustus concerning the ecstasy of Heaven.

MEPHOSTOPHILIS: Think'st thou that I who saw the face of God
    And tasted the eternal joys of heaven
    Am not tormented with ten thousand hells
    In being depriv'd of everlasting bliss? (I.iv. 78-80)

The other lesser devils whom we see are the more conventional figures, frequently portrayed in painting and carvings (particularly of the Last Judgement) as frighteningly ugly, gross animal creatures taking vicious enjoyment in driving the damned souls down to perpetual punishment in Hell. In the last moments of the play the pit of Hell is opened up before us as Faustus's body is dragged down by these fearsome devils.

But Marlowe also creates a very firm image of Heaven by his constant references to it throughout the play.

GOOD ANGEL: Sweet Faustus, think of heaven and heavenly things.
                                         (II.i.21)

FAUSTUS: When I behold the heavens then I repent,
    And curse thee, wicked Mephostophilis,
    Because thou hast depriv'd me of those joys. (II.ii. 1-3)

OLD MAN: Then thou art banish'd from the sight of heaven. (v.i. 46)

The religious concepts of damnation and salvation are treated according to contemporary theology. The Good Angel explains the 'ladder of repentance' by which salvation made be achieved.

FAUSTUS: Contrition, prayer, repentance, what of these?
ANGEL: O they are means to bring thee unto heaven. (II.i. 17-18)

Man achieved salvation, not through his own merits, but by Christ's intervention. His sacrifices as Redeemer secured the gift of mercy for all genuinely repentant sinners.

OLD MAN: O stay, good Faustus, stay thy desperate steps.
I see an angel hover o'er thy head,
And with a vial full of precious grace
Offers to pour the same into thy soul.
Then call for mercy and avoid despair. (v.i. 60-4)

Belief in God's forgiveness and mercy was an essential element in the soul's salvation. Despair, denial of or refusal to accept God's mercy, inevitably led to damnation. The verses that Faustus quotes in his dismissal of Divinity at the beginning of the play refer to this doctrine of forgiveness. He stresses the sections of the verses that refer to judgement but ignores the concluding phrases that offer forgiveness to the repentant. Theologically speaking, Faustus's damnation can be seen as the outcome of his refusal to believe in God's forgiving mercy.

3.2 *DOCTOR FAUSTUS* AS A MORALITY PLAY

Popular in medieval and Tudor times and regularly performed in schools and colleges was the 'morality' play. It was rather like a dramatised sermon, usually on the doctrine of repentance. Whilst the subject matter was serious, the presentation was often amusing, since certain characters in the play known as Vices were portrayed as lively, humorous fellows cracking vulgar jokes and singing tasteless songs. Their task was to tempt the main character from the path of virtue with all kinds of worldly delights. Other characters called Virtues, more sober and serious, would advocate repentance. The morality play usually traced the fortunes of the central character (often given a generalised name like Mankind or Everyman) in his fall from grace, through a life in sin towards eventual salvation or damnation. The Virtues, perhaps named Mercy or Wisdom, would represent salvation, whilst the Vices, with names like Mischief or Idleness strove to entice the protagonist into an evil path. Though the Vices were usually successful, the Virtues persisted in their desire to secure the soul's salvation and continued to advise and support him against the seductive delights offered by the

Vices until the moment of death. But belief in God's mercy overwhelmed the greatest sins. Even at the point of death, assertion of belief in God's mercy was sufficient for salvation. The plays that concluded in salvation were called 'merciful' moralities. However, newer Protestant theology was offering a more severe view of wrongdoing. The punished sinner was seen as an example to demonstrate God's righteous judgement and was therefore doomed to damnation. The Protestant morality plays usually concluded in a fearsome scene of destruction with the protagonist drawn down into Hell, rightfully punished.

We can recognise some of the characteristics of the morality play in *Doctor Faustus*. The virtuous figures of the Good Angel and the old man offer good advice whilst the Vice figures of the Bad Angel and Mephostophilis seek to deceive. The play covers a long span of Faustus's life in which we see him reject good advice and espouse the cause of the Devil. The conclusion of the play demonstrates damnation in horrifying spectacular detail. Lily Campbell, in an essay, 'Dr. Faustus: A Case of Conscience', has pointed out the existence of a play by Nathaniel Woodes written in 1581 called *The Conflict of Conscience*, which turns the real life story of an Italian lawyer, Francesco Spera, into a morality play with an outcome very similar to *Doctor Faustus*. The central figure, called Philologus (lover of learning), eventually commits suicide, despairing of God's forgiving mercy.

Faustus, like Philologus, is a learned, intelligent, highly esteemed academic. He can hardly be called 'Everyman'. Within him there should exist an intellectual and spiritual understanding that would enable him to resist the temptations of the Devil, knowing only too well the consequences of sinful indulgence. But this knowledge does not protect him. His ambition overrides his intellect.

CHORUS: Cut is the branch that might have grown full straight,
        And burned is Apollo's laurel bough
        That sometime grew within this learned man.
        Faustus is gone: regards his hellish fall,
        whose fiendful fortune may exhort the wise
        only to wonder at unlawful things,
        whose deepness doth entice such forward witf
        to practise more than heavenly power permits. (Epilogue 1–8)

3.3 AMBITION

E. D. Pendry, in his introduction to the *Everyman* edition of the play (1976), points out that many of the heroes of Marlowe's plays were men of intensive, even excessive, ambition. Tamburlaine sought to be a world conqueror, delighting in the destructive power that he obtained. The Jew in *The Jew of Malta*, though working on a much smaller scale, delighted in cunning manipulation of wealth. Faustus seems determined to explore the remotest possibilities of power, reaching beyond the earthly to the realms of the supernatural, magical universe. Doctor Faustus can be regarded as an ambitious, risk-taking, power seeker. He has struggled from very humble origins into a position of great eminence in the University of Wittenberg by dint of his own relentless, unremitting labours. He has acquired much-admired skills in all the great academic disciplines and could be said to be at the pinnacle of his career when the play opens. However, he is not contented with this success and desires to go further, finding a hollowness in his studies and an unsatisfied urge for further power. So he elects to break into the world of necromancy that could bring him supernatural powers and push back the frontiers of knowledge even further. There is a terrible risk in this enterprise, since black magic was universally condemned as damnable. Those who indulged in the black art gave up all hope of salvation and condemned themselves to everlasting damnation in hell. The opening chorus speaks of Faustus 'swol'n with cunning' – puffed up with his own knowledge and skill, and 'of a self conceit' – self pride. In other words, he has become arrogantly proud of his own intellectual knowledge, which leads him as the closing Chorus reminds us 'to practise more than heavenly power permits'. Faustus chooses to ignore the reservations placed on human enquiry and to reach into a forbidden realm.

The play can, therefore, be considered as a study of a man full of relentless, unabashed ambition that overreaches itself, causing the adventurer to tumble. But if we look at the pattern created in the play of Faustus's ambitious designs, a curious fact emerges. Early on we hear of grandiose schemes of world conquest – India to be ransacked for gold, Germany walled in with a brass stockade, all foreign enemies expelled. He is to be 'great emperor of the world'. As the play proceeds, we see a considerable diminution in scale of that ambition. True, the Chorus tells us of Faustus's exploits as he rides a dragon through the firmament, but what we see are tricks played on the Pope, and a series of schoolboy japes with ignorant servants and tradesmen. He also produces some very entertaining magic spectacles at the courts where he is made a welcome guest. But the exploits are of increasingly less significance and seriousness. In his last moments, Faustus is not found at the apex of his supernatural ambitions, but back in his study in Wittenberg, engaged in a debate about beautiful women.

If the play is concerned with ambition, it reveals the hollowness of that desire together with the foolish and finally tragic consequences that ensue from its thoughtless, unregarding pursuit. The play can be said to demonstrate the futility of 'vaulting ambition'.

3.4 A CHALLENGE TO THE OLD ORDER

In looking at Doctor Faustus as a morality play or as the portrait of an 'overreacher', we are aware of the religious basis to both interpretations. The first is overtly concerned with damnation, and the second demonstrates the punishment meted out for ambition that 'practises more than heavenly power permits'. In both cases the fact of damnation and heavenly authority is unchallenged. The force of the play lies in the acceptance of the inevitability of punishment in such cases. But Marlowe was writing at a time when there was considerable religious controversy and many established beliefs were being challenged. If the evidence is accepted, Marlowe personally showed extreme reluctance to accept orthodox biblical teaching uncritically. Indeed, many of his problems with the authorities appeared to arise from those challenges. The period of the English Renaissance was one of great upheaval in religious, political and moral attitudes as well as in literary and musical tastes. It is possible to see Faustus as one of the new Renaissance men exhibiting a profound discontent with the conventional past. Marlowe makes Faustus give very short shrift to the classic academic disciplines of Law, Philosophy, Medicine and Religion. He does not allow Faustus to accept the descriptions of Heaven and Hell that he is offered. He is not terrified by thoughts of damnation and to him hell belongs with the cast-off classical notions of Elysium. Marlowe causes his protagonist to risk entry to unknown and forbidden areas of exploration and experience. Men like Valdes and Cornelius seem to have discovered new, untapped sources of power, reaching beyond the natural ordered world towards supernatural supremacy that gives Man god-like pre-eminence whilst he is on earth. If such an investigation carries risks, then they are well worth taking for such a valued prize.

John Jump, in the introduction to the *Revels* edition (1962), comments: 'his ardent curiosity, his desires for wealth and luxury, and his own nationalism, as well as the longing for power, mark him unmistakably as a man of the Renaissance.' The intensity of that curiosity, the challenge to the old order, the vision of wealth and luxury combine to create a vivid, intriguing, larger than life personality with an audacity that demands admiration. But we are bound to notice that the bold political designs and supernatural adventures come to nothing. Faustus certainly achieves a god-like power, but the use to which he puts that power is steadily reduced to the trivial and superficial. Marlowe's other plays reveal his obsession with the risk-taker, the adventurer, the challenger - even when their efforts come to nothing. It may well be that this quality was the principal attraction of Faustus despite his eventual condemnation.

3.5 A PERSONAL TRAGEDY

If we look at the character of Faustus as it is created by Marlowe, we find two contrasting features dominating his personality. On the one hand there is no doubt as to his intense ambition for power and influence, but on the other, we are aware of a nagging uncertainty that develops into despair. Ambition and despair seem unlikely partners being, as they are, at opposite ends of the scale of human aspiration. Ambition can be thought of as hope stretched to its upper limit through vigorous, life-asserting, even reckless action, whilst despair epitomises hopelessness, inaction, a belief that life is no longer worth living. If ambition is seen as one face of a coin, despair can be thought of as its reverse. Ambition is bolstered by success, but how can thoughts of despair be assuaged? Faustus's life can be seen as a transition from a point where earthly knowledge and supernatural daring have lifted him to a pinnacle of success where he is 'conjuror laureate' with world-subduing power to a situation where he cries out 'Curs'd be the parents that engendered me' - intense regret at his very existence. Even in full ambitious flight sobering doubts arise. Early on Faustus says to himself 'Faustus be resolute/Why waver'st thou? O, something soundeth in mine ears' (II.i.6-7). On a later occasion of this upsurge of doubt we learn of Faustus's method of combating these unwelcome thoughts. He says:

> . . . swords and knives,
> Poison, guns, halters, and envenom'd steel
> Are laid before me to despatch myself. (II.ii. 21-23)

These are clearly instruments of self-destruction and he goes on to say:

> And long ere this I should have done the deed,
> Had not sweet pleasure conquer'd deep despair. (II.ii. 24-5)

In other words, doubts are blotted out by some diverting delight – fireworks, tricks, lavish shows or magic spectacle. It is ironic that his final conjuration, that of Helen of Troy, of whom he says:

> Here will I dwell, for heaven is in these lips,
> And all is dross that is not Helena. (v.i.104-5)

is, in fact, a conjuration of his own destroyer. The tricks on the Pope, the false heads and detachable legs, disappearing horses, and out-of-season grapes may be temporarily successful but they cannot for long repress those persistent feelings of despair. Faustus's mind is bleakly desperate. The game of chance in which the coin was spun has fallen with the reverse side uppermost. Despair has conquered ambition.

It is possible to see Faustus as a man with two contrary forces fighting within him that are incapable of co-existing. One seems bound to drive the other out. In his increasing awareness of the frightening negative influence of despair, Faustus attempts a remedy, not through extending his ambitious plans, but by increasingly desperate forays into black magic. Even if we remove the religious implications associated with ambition and despair, the psychological conflict between those two aspects of a man's personality can still be recognised. We see in *Doctor Faustus* a tragic figure caught between the extremes of readily understood impulses towards further knowledge and power and the equally well recognised force of inner uncertainties. As such he invites our sympathy and compassion. There is no joy in watching his final agony even though it could be argued that it is self inflicted and well deserved. The twin dangers of excessive ambition and despairing hopelessness remain painfully relevant to us all.

3.6 CONCLUSIONS

These varying interpretations as to what the play is about are not really contradictory. Central to them all is a man of eminent scholarship, respected by society. Hard work has raised him to a position of success and the driving force behind that energy appears to be undiminished ambition for further knowledge, enlarged power, greater authority. We may be wary but not necessarily critical of such ambition. There are, however, inbuilt dangers if this desire is carried to excess. A religious reading would show it as a challenge to God's authority. A more down-to-earth reading shows it be finally deceptive and hollow. At a personal level, the singlemindedness essential for ambition might be challenged by contradictory thoughts and feelings that resist and question the desires of ambition. However we look at it, ambition carried to excess is dangerous and often self-destructive. Deposed dictators, defeated military leaders, bankrupted business tycoons all offer examples of exploded ambition. We too are faced with this struggle for knowledge and power in a world so dangerous that the overreachers might destroy us all.

The element of despair may be interpreted as rejection of God's mercy, it could arise from a recognition of the hollowness of success, or exist as a permanently nagging feature of man's complex psychological make-up. But in every case it is negative, atrophying, and essentially destructive.

As a playwright, Marlowe searched for a dramatic form to explore a character whose complexities intrigued him, perhaps because they resembled his own. The German prose account of *Doctor Faustus* (1587) provided the basic material. Renaissance man with his eager, courageous, outward-looking, chance-taking view of the world offered a contemporary model for much that was in Marlowe's mind. The opposing tensions of good and evil contained in the formally organised morality play suggested an appropriate pattern within which to shape the action. The theological doctrines of salvation and damnation and their implications concerning unlawful ambition, merciful forgiveness and despair offered powerful religious metaphors to represent the dilemma that the protagonist faced. How may contradictions between ambition and feelings of hopelessness be resolved? Is a positive resolution possible? The play of *Doctor Faustus* is not important because of its resemblance to a morality play or the accuracy with which it handles religious concepts. Rather are these features used to dramatise the perennial dangers that face any intelligent, resourceful man of the world, eager for success at any cost. Hidden dangers, shortsightedness, psychological hazards offer an often unrecognised threat, capable of bringing down and destroying the most self-confident, self-assured human being.

Such a reading of the play places it in the main stream of tragic drama both as it relates to classical Greek heroes like Oedipus Rex and to Shakespeare's tragic heroes, such as Macbeth. Indeed, a number of critics draw comparisons between the ambition of Faustus and the ambition of Macbeth. In this sense, Doctor Faustus becomes a truly tragic hero - a man of importance, highly regarded, influential, but in whom exists a tragic flaw or defect of personality that brings about his downfall. The particular appeal of tragedy is the insight it gives us into the character of the protagonist. We can admire his learning, and yet feel fearful of his audacity. We can share the delight of his triumph and still experience compassion and fear at the awesome conclusion. These are the qualities that lift the play away from conventional moralising into a breathtaking adventure of high seriousness that takes us, as do the astronauts of our own age, beyond the known world into perilous unexplored stretches of the universe. For Faustus it went horrifically wrong. So far, modern space exploration has experienced few disasters. But the danger remains.

4 TECHNICAL FEATURES

4.1 PLOT AND STRUCTURE

The source material from which Marlowe constructs *Doctor Faustus* consists of a miscellaneous collection of stories and anecdotes contained in *The Damnable Life*. Tales about George Faustus stress his long addiction to necromancy rather than his scholarship. He was famed as an itinerant magician wandering through Europe entertaining and amazing all with his marvellous conjurations. Now Marlowe certainly uses several events reported in *The Damnable Life* in his own play, for instance the conjuration of Mephostophilis, details of the contract with Lucifer, some of the debates, the fun with the Pope, the magical appearance of Alexander, the jokes with the deer horns and the horse dealer, the grapes for the Duchess of Vanholt, the episode with Helen and the horrifying end. But whilst the German narrative emphasises the amazement and the spectacle, Marlowe gives his John Faustus a far more serious, tragic personality. The events are ordered into a careful dramatic pattern created (a) by the Chorus and (b) by the time scheme.

The Chorus gives a formal shape to the pattern of the play with the Prologue, the Epilogue and the two intervening choruses. The Prologue introduces the audience to Faustus and the precise nature of his defection, whilst the two choruses act as stepping stones on the journey taking us first to Rome and then back to Germany. The concluding admonition, in the style of a morality play epilogue warns the audience to take heed of the dreadful example they have just witnessed. Overlaying that formal pattern is a carefully devised time scheme. The contract with Lucifer requires a time span of twenty-four years. Chronologically the play can be seen to have a short opening section culminating in the powerful and dramatic signing of the contract, an extended middle section where the various exploits necessarily occupy a longer time span and the final section swiftly introduced by the student's remark 'I think my master means to die shortly' (v.i.1). The opening and closing sequences take place in Faustus's study, while the intervening section – to reinforce the suggestion of a longer period of time – moves through various locations: Rome, the court of Emperor Charles and the dukedom of Vanholt. By using this time pattern, Marlowe creates two peaks (the contract and the condemnation) joined by less intense sections where Faustus's sardonic wit tempers the seriousness.

This reasonably straightforward framework is complicated by interleaving with Faustus's various enterprises, the exploits of his servants and a group of country yokels. These episodes not only provide a rough comic relief to the more serious events, they also offer an ironic parody of the main plot through the comic conjurations that contrast vividly with Faustus's necromancy. By containing the comedy principally within the middle section, Marlowe avoids detracting from the seriousness of the major dramatic episodes. However, he prevents the transition being too abrupt by his early introduction of the servants. The careful combination of high tragedy, impressive spectacle and low comedy succeeds in maintaining a continuing interest in and attention to the play. We are never sure what will happen next even though we are aware of what the final outcome will be.

Although Faustus is undoubtedly an intelligent and learned man, we notice from the very first how Mephostophilis and, later, Lucifer manipulate his thoughts and actions. They are quick to spot the dangerous moments when the discussion becomes too serious and they speedily offer diversions or distractions to which Faustus inevitably succumbs. It is the dramatic encounter between these three figures that establishes the serious centre of the play. Their exchanges can never be taken lightly. We may laugh at the antics of the lesser devils with their fireworks and noisy interruptions but Mephostophilis and Lucifer must always be held in wary respect. Marlowe creates forceful and subtle characters out of these infernal adversaries.

The structure of the main plot of *Doctor Faustus* may, most easily, be thought of in three sections. The first is concerned with the acquisition of power, the second, the experience of power and the third with the final hours of Faustus's life. We can see that alongside that main plot is a subsidiary one involving a group of servants whose exploits mirror the principal events, until, eventually, they too become absorbed into the main plot.

The acquisition of power

Having discarded the recognised areas of academic study, Faustus determines to follow necromancy, a black, forbidden, magic art. He holds discussions with two notorious black magicians, Valdes and Cornelius, learning from them the various procedures by which the Devil may be conjured. This knowledge acquired, Faustus quickly sets about the task and believes that he has been successful in causing the appearance of Mephostophilis. He does not approve of Mephostophilis's dragon-like appearance and the devilish figure is required to reappear in the guise of a Franciscan friar. Negotiations begin, and the transaction is completed by the signing of a deed of gift in which Faustus promises to give his soul and body to Lucifer in exchange for a period of twenty-four years during which Mephostophilis will be entirely at the command of Faustus, who himself will become 'a spirit in form and substance' (endowed with extraordinary power). Faustus has swiftly accomplished his desire and is full of ideas as to how he will use this new-found omnipotence. However, the process is not quite so simple as has been described. At the same time that Faustus moves upward on his ambitious path, grave misgivings are experienced as to the sense of his decision. His own young scholars are quick to recognise the dangers of dealing with Valdes and Cornelius. The appearance of the Good and Bad Angels draw a question mark over Faustus's actions. The Good Angel is anxious to deflect him from these devilish practices. Even Mephostophilis adds his recommendation to Faustus to 'leave off these frivolous demands'. The congealing of his blood and the appearance of the words '*Homo fuge*' imprinted on his arm are further warnings to Faustus of the hazards attached to his ambitious plan. Thus it is very clear from the outset that the course Faustus has elected to follow invites damnation. He steadfastly rejects the warnings, even if, temporarily, he is uneasily aware of them. But this is not all. The boundless power that he believes he has secured is soon revealed to have several limitations. The very appearance of Mephostophilis was not as a direct result of his skilful conjuration. Mephostophilis always has one ear cocked for blasphemy, offering, as it does, another possible candidate for hell. When he asks for a wife, the request is refused and instead he is offered 'a hot whore'. The questions he poses to Mephostophilis are not always answered in full. Indeed, some receive no satisfactory answer at all. In total these limitations represent a severe reduction of the power for which he has exchanged his soul and body. Faustus, uncomfortably aware of some misgivings and of the prompting of the Good Angel, and recognising the threat of damnation, is persuaded out of his disquiet by a series of diversions: gifts of rich garments, books of astronomy and natural science and, following the intervention of Lucifer, a spectacular show of the Seven Deadly Sins. Faustus is duly delighted and his uncertainties are temporarily assuaged.

The experience of power

The Chorus tells of Faustus's various exploits on his magic chariot through the heavens, but we actually see Faustus with Mephostophilis in Rome when, through a series of tricks, they secure the release of the captive Bruno, throw the Pope's banquet into complete disarray and chase the chanting friars with fireworks. It must be admitted that amusing though these escapades are, they hardly relate to the ambitious plans that Faustus spoke of earlier. But the light-hearted tone continues. The Chorus tells of Faustus's return to Germany and we hear of further comic exploits with Benvolio, the horse dealer and other servants. The magic produces out-of-season grapes. Faustus also conjures, at the request of the Emperor, a splendid dumb show that dramatises Alexander's defeat of Darius. This feat is much admired by the onlookers, but, again, it must be seen as a serious reduction in the aim and scope of Faustus's immense power.

We should, perhaps, notice that throughout this section of the play we see nothing of the Good and Bad Angels and there is only one brief scene, carefully inserted to remind us of the spiritual background, in which Faustus expresses feelings of despair. The period of power is principally a joyful romp of less than serious impact. The overall sense is of frivolous misuse of power. It has already been mentioned that Marlowe may not have been the author of these scenes, which accounts for the clearly different tone, but on the other hand the section could be regarded as a bitterly ironic comment on Faustus's experience of power. Marlowe would also have enjoyed the mocking attack on the dignity of the Pope.

The final hours

A sombre, serious tone marks the final hours of Faustus's life. Feelings of desperate melancholy gain ascendancy. In a subdued conversation with his students, Faustus conjures the spirit of Helen of Troy and after the students' departure seeks to drown his sorrows in her loving embrace. But the renowned, beautiful Helen is shown to be a female devil. Her kiss draws out his soul, never to be recovered. This last conjuration is the beginning of Faustus's own destruction. Desperate though he feels, the possibility of salvation has not completely passed. The Old Man and the Good Angel urge him towards repentance, but following the episode with Helen, they realise the time for contrition is over. In this last sequence we see Faustus's increasing melancholy which he cannot shake off. He reveals to his concerned students the details of the devilish contract. The last hour is a powerful, painful exposure of his deepest personal feelings. He desires to hold back time, to sink into the earth, to dissolve in mist, smoke or water drops. Powerfully evoked are visions of Christ's merciful blood streaming in the heavens and, finally, the fierce figure of the God of Judgement as the devils rise from Hell to drag his soul into perpetual torment. As the students prepare the mangled body for decent burial, so the Chorus comes forward with a solemn warning against enticement 'to practise more than heavenly power permits'.

The subsidiary plot

A second story concerning a group of servants and workmen runs parallel to the main plot until eventually these characters participate in the events of the main plot. The servants are also involved in conjuring on an amateur scale with exciting but not too dangerous results. First we meet Wagner, the quick-witted servant of Faustus. He needs further assistance and bullies or cajoles Robin, the would-be employee, with a display of conjuring. He actually produces two devils and Robin wants to learn the secrets. Next Robin attempts some conjurations to show off his skill to Dick, the ostler. In attempting to deceive a vintner the pair invoke the aid of Mephostophilis. He is far from pleased to be called away from serious duties for this frivolous activity and metes out punishment to the hapless servants. At this point they are drawn into the main plot which involves the horse-dealer and the carter and they all end up by being struck dumb by Faustus. They are not seen in the final sequence of the play.

The effect of the subsidiary plot is to provide a comic commentary on the main story. The servants manage a number of magic tricks from what they have picked up from Faustus or overheard of his actions. Conjuring is not so difficult after all if such menials can do it. Their experiments are lightly regarded but when they threaten to get out of hand, Mephostophilis steps in and stops any further frivolity. However, unlike Faustus, they do not exchange their souls for the skills they acquire. The comic tone that they introduce into the play is entirely absent from the final act.

4.2 CHARACTERISATION

One of the notable features of the play is the rich variety of characters that are introduced by the author. They range from popes, emperors, kings and courtiers to servants, tradesmen and country folk. We are also confronted with supernatural beings: Lucifer, Belzebub, and, in particular, the Devil's emissary, Mephostophilis. These, together with a group of attendant devils, engage in the action of the play. There is also a further group of spirits: some speaking, like the Seven Deadly Sins; others silent, like Alexander and Helen. Two angels offer advice, as does an unnamed old man. In all, Marlowe offers samples from every stratum of society, from the most elevated to the most base. Whilst few are seen on more than one occasion, nevertheless they create a vivid dramatic impression which animates the scenes in which they take part.

Doctor Faustus

The principal figure in the play is, of course, Doctor Faustus: scholar, magician, 'insatiable speculator'. We know his character was derived from a real historical figure, but the play is not simply a dramatisation of the 'historie'. The playwright uses only what is convenient to his purpose, adding or excluding incidents as thought fit: Faustus in the play must be regarded as Marlowe's own creation.

He is unquestionably a learned academic, holding an important post in the University of Wittenberg, having reached that eminence by his own industry and scholarship. Faustus demonstrates a wide-ranging knowledge of many academic studies, including Law and Medicine as well as Divinity for which he is awarded a doctorate. He is held in considerable respect by his students, who show a great concern for him at the beginning and end of the play. So far as scholarship is concerned, Faustus seems to have reached a pinnacle of success which would content many men, yet leaves him unsatisfied.

Much of the character of Faustus is exposed in two ways: the particular traits of personality he reveals and the tensions that they produce within his personality. A similar tension is shown in the way that Faustus uses his power. It is the combination of these outward actions and inner stresses that create the complex character of the protagonist.

Dominating his personality is intense ambition, pride, 'self conceit' that desires greater power than he already possesses. He wants omnipotence:

> A sound magician is a demi-god.
> Here, Faustus, try thy brains to get a deity. (I.i.63-4)

These lines indicate also a second feature of his personality. He is ready to take risks, to use all his energies to explore what he knows to be forbidden territory. He is ready 'to practise more than heavenly power permits'. Intense ambition, and unceasing, inquisitive energy combine to make the forceful driving element of Faustus's character. Set against and in conflict with this energy are two other characteristics. Despite his go-ahead certainty, there exists within Faustus a troubling conscience that will never leave him entirely at his ease. Interleaved with the scenes of intense activity, debate, splendid conjuration are still moments when his conscience asserts itself and he questions the validity of his actions. We may think that the Good Angel and the Old Man personify that conscience, but in any event, it is inescapably present despite all Faustus's attempts to push it into the background. We should note that he ignores the specific advice offered by the Good Angel, even though he has been given clear indications as to the prospects of damnation. He asserts that he is not terrified by damnation or thoughts of Hell. This is in spite of the clear evidence proffered by Mephostophilis and the realisation present in the minds of his own pupils. This shortsightedness, refusal to countenance uncomfortable evidence and rejection of unequivocal advice creates in Faustus what D. J. Palmer (in 'Magic and Poetry in *Dr. Faustus*') calls 'hubristic blindness,' a stubborn refusal to acknowledge what Fate (or God) will use to bring about your eventual downfall. Such a characteristic should be totally alien to a learned scholar. This troubled conscience and 'blindness' combine to combat or negate the positive elements of ambition and energy. The tension they create is what eventually destroys him.

Another kind of tension is observed when we consider Faustus's use of his power. At first, we hear of heroic ideas of world-changing stature:

> All things that move between the quiet poles
> Shall be at my command.   (i.i.56–7)

To achieve this domination he enters into a contract with Lucifer, acquiring power, but at extreme cost – the loss of his soul. His discourses with Mephostophilis consist of scholarly argument ranging through the whole universe, and we also hear of his space journey on a dragon's back when he makes an aerial survey of the whole world. From that point onward, however, a significant change occurs from grandiloquence to petty magic. Certainly he secures the release of Bruno, but the remainder of his sojourn in the Holy City is taken up with japes played on the Pope and his friars. He conducts a 'royal' progress through the courts of Europe, but Germany is not 'walled up with brass' nor does the 'swift Rhine encircle fair Wittenberg'. Instead we are presented with a sophisticated series of conjuring tricks, and magical manifestations of heroes and heroines of the past. The only courtier who is not impressed by this show is dealt with very harshly. There are further vulgar jokes with false heads and legs and disappearing horses. We move from grandeur to bathos. In the last conjuration, that of Helen, Faustus initiates the final phase of his life. The beautiful spirit is, in fact, a devil in disguise who 'sucks forth' his soul. What a tremendous contrast exists between those initial intentions and the increasingly sordid, if amusing, use to which that power is actually put. This distinction between intention and execution illuminates a gradually disintegrating personality. The criminal becomes the victim. Interwoven with the series of exploits are regular reminders of his own mortality. There is a tension between achievement and doubt. The initial self-assurance and energetic fooling is eroded to leave increasing self-questioning, regret, even a desire for self-destruction.

Thus we can see that Marlowe has created an intensely complex character. He is at once learned and shortsighted, heroic and trivial, fearless and conscience-ridden, ambitious and foolish. He may well typify the Renaissance man, well equipped to search for new horizons, yet he is destroyed by a bargain which, for his part, is scarcely worthwhile.

Mephostophilis

Doctor Faustus is not a one-character play. Marlowe has created in the character of Mephostophilis a compelling, powerful figure whose personality is far from simple. In status he is a fallen angel ejected from Heaven with Lucifer. He brings into the play a personal experience of Heaven as well as the knowledge of the agony of expulsion and existence in Hell. With this knowledge of Mephostophilis, we must regard what he says about Heaven and Hell with some care. In the play he portrays the faithful representative of Satan, always referring back to his master, greatly aware of the conditions and limitations associated with the legal contract. We notice his constant fidelity to the Luciferan law. Following his conjuration we are reminded of his ubiquitous presence, apparently summoned, but in fact always on watch and alert for any soul inviting damnation.

This characterisation makes Mephostophilis a sinister, dangerous figure with immensely powerful resources. At first his actual appearance is frightening as he erupts on to the stage as a fearful dragon, but he quickly transforms himself into a Franciscan friar, apparently humble, obedient and respectful. This 'obedience' is totally misleading. In turn, during the play, we see Mephostophilis as tempter, servant, disputant, conjurer's assistant and finally as an agent of destruction. From the beginning, with his *'per accidens'* reference, we know what his true intention is - to capture the soul of Faustus. Much later in the play he confesses to manipulating the Bible pages so that Faustus might draw the wrong conclusions from the passages of Scripture. So Mephostophilis is undoubtedly the tempter, but he appears to be the servant and the terms of his servitude are clearly expressed in the deed of gift: Mephostophilis is to be the servant of Faustus, at his command, constantly on hand to 'do for him and bring him whatsoever', invisibly present at all times, ready to appear at whatever time and in whatever form he is required. He conforms to these requirements only insofar as they suit him. In disputation with Faustus he readily answers all the questions about Hell, but is reluctant to discuss 'who made the world'. When Faustus asks for a wife he is provided with a woman devil sprouting fireworks. As to questions on astrology, Faustus already knows much of the information. So the subjugation of Mephostophilis to Faustus is more apparent than real. However we cannot ignore that powerful, passionate remonstrance made by Mephostophilis early in the play when he urges:

> O Faustus, leave these frivolous demands,
> Which strike a terror to my fainting soul. (ɪ.iv. 81-2)

Perhaps it is an expression of momentary pity, but it does stress the immensity of the risk that Faustus is taking. In the passage from which the above quotation comes we have a vivid picture of the true nature of Mephostophilis, the torment and agony that he suffers in Hell.

> Think'st thou that I who saw the face of God
> And tasted the eternal joys of heaven
> Am not tormented with ten thousand hells
> In being depriv'd of everlasting bliss? (ɪ.iv. 77-80)

His only joy now is seeing the torment and torture of others: *Solamen miseris socios habuisse dolaris* - 'to the unhappy it is a comfort to have companions in misfortune'.

Faustus has allied himself to a once powerful, now rejected Angel who recognises only too clearly the error that Faustus so lightheartedly makes. But having uttered his warning, Mephostophilis continues to aid his 'master' in his various designs, enjoying the partnership in crime, the escapades in Rome, producing the grapes - but showing a sudden burst of irritation with Robin and Dick when they call him from more important duties. Mephostophilis begins as a devilish archangel, then becomes a conjuror's assistant, but his last role is as an agent of destruction. It is Mephostophilis who sraws the devilish Helen on to the stage. It is he who offers a dagger to a despairing Faustus close to suicide. He openly admits his earlier deceptions and exults in Faustus's desperation:

I do confess it, Faustus, and rejoice.
'Twas I that, when thou wert i' the way to heaven,
Damned up thy passage; when thou took'st the book
To view the scriptures, then I turn'd the leaves
And led thine eye.
What, weep'st thou? 'Tis too late, despair. Farewell.
Fools that will laugh on earth, must weep in hell. (v.ii. 93-9)

In stressing the intensity of their relationship, the subtlety of the deception, the shared schoolboy jokes, Marlowe creates a vivid companion for Faustus, one from whom we would wish to remain warily distant, but whom Faustus welcomes as a co-operative conspirator and companion, realising too late the fatal nature of their fellowship.

Subsidiary characters

No other characters are seen in such depth as Faustus and Mephostophilis. The popes, emperors, kings and courtiers serve only as agents through whom Faustus can show his necromantic skills. Marlowe daringly creates the Pope and his dining companions as figures of fun. All their pomposity is punctured. The Emperor and the Vanholts are merely mystified onlookers enjoying the spectacles that Faustus stage-manages. None of these courtly celebrities can be taken seriously, but they do provide a rich background of elaborate ceremonial and splendid pageantry which Faustus can enjoy in his mischievous moods.

The servants, too, are usually dupes. In their comic antics and boasting they exhibit a selfish desire to benefit from magic, though they seldom reach beyond cheating, getting free drinks or misguided deals in horses or hay. Wagner, Faustus's servant, shows a certain quick-wittedness but the others are generally dull-brained, easily fooled country bumpkins.

The third category of characters, the spirits and apparitions, give another dimension to the play. The low-born devils with fireworks supply a boisterous comic tone: they need not be taken too seriously. The same cannot be said for Lucifer and his companions. These are a dangerous, menacing group, sharply observant, keenly intelligent, possessed of supernatural power, unseen but inescapable. It is worth noting the moment when Lucifer makes his personal presence felt. It follows the expression of strong doubts by Faustus. Then the Devil decides to take a hand in the proceedings lest his victim escapes. Marlowe allows us to laugh at the comic devils but not at the principal agents of darkness.

The display of the Seven Deadly Sins is a clear reminder of the medieval morality plays which were full of such characters. Though each of the figures is formally named as a Sin, each presents a sharp portrait of indulgent humanity with an all too human face. They are uncomfortably near to ourselves. The classic conqueror Alexander shows more dignity than his human counterparts. The spectacle of Alexander prepares us for the conjuration of another classic figure, Helen of Troy, dignified in her destructiveness, sublimely beautiful but utterly deadly. These shows so greatly extend the range of characterisation that the scale on which Faustus operates clearly transcends the ordinary. Deeper levels of existence are reached through the supernatural and classic past. Taken altogether, the subsidiary characters are lively, vividly drawn, richly various, diverse in nature and form. They enliven the scenes in which they appear and act as suitable foils for the main protagonist. Each enables a certain facet of the character of Faustus to be revealed: his ambition, his necromantic skills, his irritations, his foolishness and his despair.

4.3 STYLE AND LANGUAGE

The excitement and freshness of Marlowe's writing lies in the richness of his language and innovative poetic style. His poetry in blank verse, compelling in its vividness, intensifies the dramatic action. His dramatic poetry is essentially 'language in action'.

Marlowe's own contemporaries were full of admiration for his literary accomplishments. Ben Jonson referred in a poem praising William Shakespeare to 'Marlowe's mighty line'. Another Elizabethan poet, Michael Drayton, spoke of his poetry being 'All ayre and fire which made his verses cleare'. So persuasively did Marlowe develop the blank verse form that it came to dominate much of Elizabethan and Jacobean playwriting. Shakespeare employed and continued to refine the use of blank verse in his own great tragedies.

Blank verse consists of lines on non-rhyming poetry, each line normally having ten syllables with alternate weak and strong stress. The form had already been used by a poet, the Earl of Surrey, and playwrights Norton and Sackville in their drama *Gorbuduc*. But it was Marlowe who developed the form, employing intense poetic skill and dramatic imagination. He was very critical of his immediate playwriting predecessors who composed in heavily stressed, rhyming couplets, often little better than doggerel.

Though freed from an obvious rhyming pattern, blank verse with its regular beat and lines of equal length (technically called iambic pentameters) can be monotonous. The regular rhythm with its marching beat gives the verse strength and continuous forward movement, but unless some variations within the line are attempted, the whole effect can be very dull. It is in those modifications that Marlowe's poetic genius is revealed. He uses the even stress to give a strong dynamic rhythm, but introduces into that basic pattern a whole range of variations that break up, or modify, the evenness of the verse.

He contrasts words of one syllable (monosyllabic) with words having many syllables (polysyllabic). One line might consist solely of one or two syllable words: 'The end of physic is our body's pain', whilst others employ mainly polysyllabic words: 'And thousand desperate maladies been cured'. Lines may begin with short words and then half-way through change to longer words: 'When Mars did mate' (all monosyllabic) is completed by 'the warlike Carthagens' (one, then two, then three syllabled words). The regular thump of the first half, emphasised by the alliteration of 'Mars' and 'mate', is softened by the less obvious rhythm of the second part of the line.

A break (caesura) introduced within a line, dividing it into two sections, shows a natural pause in the speaking of the line – 'Having commenced, be a divine in show', while 'Thou art a spirit: God cannot pity thee' presents two separate ideas in one line.

Though the meaning of the text seldom runs beyond the length of one line (end-stopped lines), Marlowe frequently commences the following line with 'and', 'but', 'yet' so that the lines are linked together in a continuous chain, and the flow of thoughts being explored is maintained. This device is technically called *parataxis*. The effect is an accumulation of different ideas sometimes rather loosely linked, but nevertheless sweeping the listener along because of the excitement and colour of the language and images.

Marlowe also uses question and answer. One character might ask a question in one line and the following line would be a response to it. 'Did not he change thee to appear to me?/No, I came hither of mine own accord'. Here the blank verse appears to assume the style of natural conversation. Some lines are abrupt commands – 'I charge thee to return and change thy shape.' (Note the alliteration of 'charge' and 'change' and of 'thee' and 'thy'.) In contrast other lines are full of self-concern and uncertainty: 'My senses are deceived, here's nothing writ.' (Note the break after 'deceived' and the hardness of the concluding 'writ' compared with the softer sounds of 'senses' and 'deceived').

Repetitions of words or phrases intensify their urgency:

> FAUSTUS: Where are you damn'd?
> MEPHOSTOPHILIS: In hell.
> FAUSTUS: How comes it then that thou art out of hell?
> MEPHOSTOPHILIS: Why, this is hell, nor I am I out of it.

The vigorous question and answer exchange between Faustus and Mephostophilis reiterates 'hell' three times in three lines. (The previous four lines have repeated 'Lucifer'.) In his final speech Faustus cries: 'My God, my God! Look not so fierce on me!' Occasionally the regular iambic rhythm is changed by an alteration of stress: 'Damn'd be this soul for ever for this deed'. 'Damn'd' is strong rather than weak, but the regular stress is recovered by the end of the line.

The 'mightiness' of Marlowe's lines is not only derived from his skilful manipulation of the blank verse form, but also in his marvellous use of figurative language. The richness of his vocabulary, the vividness of his imagery and the immense range of his literary references and allusions combine to create poetry that is energetic, outgoing, and stimulating. Words are chosen for their active movement, expansiveness and vigour. Metaphor, simile, hyperbole, with frequent references to the classical gods and heroes, lift the verse from the commonplace to a world of movement, excitement, boundless in its horizons. So the large-scale canvas stretches from Heaven to Hell and includes all the regions in between, both classical and Christian. We find reference to exotic places, earthly riches, great rivers, soaring mountains and deep chasms. The listener's imagination is constantly stirred by the unusual, the surprising, the challenging, even the shocking nature of what Marlowe seeks to express in his poetry.

Impressive though Marlowe's writing is as poetry we must also notice its dramatic significance. It is easy to get carried away by the magnificent flow of the language and ignore the dramatic action that it accompanies. The play is, of course, full of action (conjuring, spectacle, spurting fireworks, menacing or comic devils and the amusing antics of the servants) but even in the quieter sections and long soliloquies, there is a powerful evocation of mood and feeling that animates the characters' actions and responses. The poetry is essentially dramatic, reaching full fruition in performance.

Some examples may help to illustrate Marlowe's style and language in detail.

The Prologue immediately sets the tone of the whole play. A large-scale historical and geographical landscape is created, filled out with classical allusions. Mention is made of the great military victories of the Carthaginian general, Hannibal, whose ally is no less than Mars, the god of war. Next mentioned is Edward II's intimate friendship with his beloved courtier, Gaveston, where 'sporting in the dalliance of love' brings about the fall of Kings. 'The pomp and proud audacious deeds' refers to the exploits of world conqueror Tamburlaine. (Edward and Tamburlaine had already been subjects for Marlowe's tragic writing.) Such vivid, bold, far-reaching references set up an expectation that seems immediately to be contradicted. These are *not* the scenes we are about to witness. The tone quietens temporarily and we learn of Faustus's parentage and scholarly leanings. Gradually, however, the tempo increases and the poetic images link Faustus with the Greek mythological figure of Icarus who fell to his death in the sea. The wax that affixed wings to his body melted during a daring attempt at flying which took him too close to the sun and to his destruction. The events we are about to witness are greater and more dangerous than those associated with Hannibal or Tamburlaine. 'Swollen', 'glutted' self-conceit will bring about the downfall of one whom 'learning's golden gifts' have lifted to great heights. The subject is not world domination but eternal damnation. Earthly locations like Italy and Germany give place to Heaven and Hell. The words challenge and excite. We hear of 'audacious', 'cunning', 'surfeit' contrasting with more thoughtful references to 'heavenly', 'fruitful', 'golden', 'bliss'. The prologue begins with general wide-ranging allusions and finishes with the central figure at the particular moment that begins the play.

The Prologue provides apt examples of Marlowe's manipulation of the blank verse form. We notice the single-syllable words that dominate the final line: 'And this the man that in his study sits'. Earlier, examples are found of flowing, polysyllabic phrases: 'Excelling all, and sweetly can dispute/ In the heavenly matters of theology.' We also find a caesura in mid line and, unusually, the meaning continuing beyond the line end: 'Only this, gentlemen: we must perform/The form of Faustus' fortunes, good or bad.' (Note also the repetition of the word 'form', the alliteration, the vowel assonance in 'form' and 'fortune' and the antithesis of 'good': 'bad'. Indeed the word 'form' has an impact on the ear in three ways, by its repetition, by its alliteration and in its vowel assonance which is continued in 'fortunes'. There is also a subtle stress change in the first half of the line.) Marlowe uses the linking words 'Not' and 'Nor' in the first part of the speech and 'And' in the latter part to connect the various sections of the prologue together. It begins with reference to other plays that Marlowe has written, moves on to Faustus's biography and then announces the subject of this particular play.

It is the prolific and subtle combination of all these rhythmic and figurative elements that makes Marlowe's verse so strong, flexible and imaginative. Dramatically speaking the broad, wide-ranging references that open the play are carefully narrowed down to focus on the protagonist. Having been given a vivid portrait of this conceited theologian, embarked on 'devilish exercises', the audience is invited into the very study in which the dangerous doctor is ensconced. Already excitement is high and the air filled with a mixture of expectation and fear as to what we are going to witness.

Marlowe's finest work is found in Faustus's long soliloquies. In the speech beginning 'My heart is hard'ned; I cannot repent' (II.ii 18–32) and the debate that follows, we see excellent examples of his poetic devices and fertile imagination. Lines full of short-syllabled words: 'And long are this I should have done the deed' (note alliteration of 'done' and 'deed') contrast with the more complex words of a line like: 'With ravishing sound of his melodious harp'. The sharp drum beat of the former counterpoints the softer, more flexible sound (and sense) of 'ravishing' and 'melodious'. The opening assertion supplies a caesura. We see the thought process joined by 'And long' (24) and 'And hath' (28). 'Faustus thou art damn'd' offers a bold statement. The question 'Why should I die then, or basely despair?' (note slightly changed stress) Faustus answers for himself with an exhortation, 'Faustus shall not repent'. These eighteen lines aptly illustrate the method Marlowe uses to vary the basic blank verse form. The principal contrasts in the passage, however, lie between the *suicidal despair* with which the speech commences and the *pleasure* that is employed to subdue it. The despair is emphasised by a fearful list of actual weapons of destruction–swords, knives, poison, guns, halters, poisoned daggers. There is no escaping their frightening reality. A horrific voice 'thunders' inside his head insisting on his damnation. The antidote to these noises is to seek refuge in the realms of mythology. Balm is found in the great Greek poet Homer's songs of the noble heroes like Paris (son of Priam, called Alexander by Homer) and his lover Oenone, or of Amphion whose 'ravishing' music caused stones to form themselves into the walls of Thebes. These images rise above mortal existence into fanciful hyperbole: he has made Homer sing for him. Re-creating the exploits of the heroes of antiquity has successfully conquered his feelings of suicide with sensuous pleasure. Words like 'repentance', 'salvation', 'faith' and 'heaven' are blotted out by the 'thunder' of damnation. We have a sense of the terrible war being waged in Faustus's mind. Relief is possible only through escapism, through conjuration. But resolution halts the challenging, contradictory, thoughts and Faustus turns back to formal disputation with Mephostophilis.

These next exchanges offer further illustrations of Marlowe's style. In a formal disputation, the speakers alternate with challenge and response, question and answer. Here Marlowe sometimes makes the dialogue brisk with short, one-line exchanges. At other times the questions and explanations are rather longer. The discussion on 'divine astrology' takes us into outer space with questions about the motions of the planets, truths and fables concerning the universe. The talk is as between two intelligent scientists. The language is precise, scientific and technical with little elaboration or imagery. But the conversation is brought to an abrupt end when Faustus asks directly, 'Who made the world?' This indiscreet enquiry changes the mood. The quick question receives a swift rebuff, forcing Faustus to turn his mind back to what, earlier, he had avoided – the question of repentance.

The sequence also demonstrates 'language in action' particularly as it relates to the feelings and the changing mood that give a dramatic shape to the whole scene. Faustus's debate with himself moves from the horror of suicide to the pleasurable thoughts by which they are overcome. Then he takes a brisk decision against repentance and the dramatic mood changes to energetic discussion. However this is less than satisfactory. Some answers given by Mephostophilis reflect commonplace knowledge. When an answer to 'Who made the world?' is denied, Faustus becomes angry at the refusal. Mephostophilis quickly retorts, 'Thou art damn'd, think thou of hell'. The wheel has come full circle. That despair which Faustus wanted to forget in pleasure pours back into his mind, and the full tide of distress sweeps over him, precipitating the arrival of the Good and Bad Angels. The mood of Faustus moves from despair to assurance, to discontent, to anger and back to despair. Mephostophilis, apparently benevolent and responsive, quickly adopts a sharp denunciatory tone when the awkward question is asked. The style and tone of the language employed in a variety of forms (for example, the scientific discussion is in prose) is closely related to and reflects the dramatic shape of the whole sequence.

The lyrical beauty and tragic grandeur of the speech in praise of Helen has always been much admired. If we look closely at the passage, however, we see that it moves in two opposing directions. Marlowe has created an ironic conflict between the exquisite language and the dramatic action that accompanies it.

At her first appearance before the scholars Faustus remained silent, but at her second entry his words evoke her beauty and the glory of the Trojan war. The gathering of the powerful Greek fleet and the terrible sacking of Troy stem from events at which she was the centre. Such was the power of her attraction. Marlowe makes the metaphor very direct: 'her face' launched the thousand ships, 'her face' destroyed Troy. Such was the mighty influence of 'sweet Helen'. Faustus compares himself with Paris 'sacking', 'combating', 'wounding' for the sake of Helen. He aligns himself with the great generals performing deeds of valour, destruction and conquest. This hyperbolic image mounts even higher to include the Greek Pantheon. Helen is *fairer* than 'a thousand stars', *brighter* than Jupiter whose dazzling fire destroyed Semele, *lovelier* than the sun god whose brilliance was reflected in the waters of the nymph Arethusa's spring. These comparisons (in which Helen is always superior to the gods) pile one upon another into a paean of extravagant praise. D. J. Palmer (in 'Magic and Poetry in *Dr Faustus*') writes 'Faustus' poetry invests Helen and himself with mythological splendour; it lifts them into another dimension of illusion, and clothes the nakedness of the stage.'

Ironically Semele and Arethusa were victims of love, but Marlowe has inserted a greater irony into the extended Greek allusion. The first three lines are immensely evocative – the 'thousand ships', 'the topless towers' speak of strength and infinite power. Faustus draws this paragon of beauty into an embrace. But the outcome is stupendous. The following abrupt, single-syllable line announces, 'Her lips suck forth my soul, see where it flies'. We may note the monosyllabic tone; the alliteration of 'suck', 'soul' and 'see'; observe the caesura that divides the two halves of the line; but dramatically an event of horrific significance has taken place. The glamorous Helen is, in fact, a female devil in disguise who actually draws out his soul. She represents false sensual beauty for which he has given up his chance of salvation. Though couched in exotic, sensual terms that embrace is deadly; an act by which Faustus denies himself the grace of Heaven. All the hyperbole of the language is in direct contrast to the event we witness, deluding in its beauty. Confirmation of the irony is immediately achieved by the entry of the Old Man who, after earlier appeals, now denounces Faustus: 'Accursed Faustus, miserable man,/That from thy soul exclud'st the grace of heaven'. We notice the abrupt change in the tone and beat of the line from the preceding words that spoke of 'wanton Arethusa's azur'd arms' and Helen as Faustus's 'paramour'.

This passage is an example of Marlowe's mighty lines, superb, evocative, beautiful, providing a contrasting dramatic dimension by virtue of the actions that they imply. As Faustus, in a flourish of extravagant praise embraces Helen, seeking 'heaven' in her lips, he is, at that moment, confirming his passage to Hell.

The cosmic dimension into which Faustus so readily moves in soliloquies and conversations about the stars and the universe acquires an awful reality in his final speech. A desperate attempt to delay the passage of time with the strong, ongoing rhythm of the striking clock is made by demands of 'Stand still', 'cease', 'never come'. But the verse moves relentlessly forward to Faustus's confrontation with the vision of Christ whose merciful blood he sees streaming 'in the firmament' and the fierce face of the God of Judgement. This terrifying spectacle is followed by a desire for deliverance from damnation. Marlowe creates a series of 'escape' images: holes in the earth, enclosure in clouds, transformation into an animal, transmutation into droplets of water lost in a waste of water; but all are useless. An appeal for clemency is followed by a curse upon his parents. Then the focus somersaults from Heaven to 'adders and serpents' of ugly, gaping Hell. Here the force of the final speech is intensified by what we observe of Faustus in his dying moments. The words are not simply poetic excursions into the fabulist worlds of the past or questions for theological debate but heartrendingly direct: Marlowe places us with Faustus in his agony. We do not observe from a distance. What he is experiencing is real. Hell is actually staring him in the face. His foolish pact now acquires a horrible, physical reality as the truth and consequence of what he has done becomes inescapable. The poetic devices and theatrical effects combine to make a conclusion of tragic dimensions. The blank verse is broken again and again by caesura. The rhythmic pattern is so manipulated that it gives the effect of direct speech with pauses, hesitations, repetitions, ending in cries of despair and disintegration. The verse form remains constant to the end but it is so skilfully managed that we are aware not only of the driving beat, but also of the human agony contained in the actual utterance.

Marlowe has jettisoned all the cumbersome, labouring rhymes and rhythms of the earlier plays. He has produced a vibrant, outward-looking, yet disciplined verse form that becomes the most prominent with his contemporaries and successors.

The play is not entirely in blank verse. Several scenes make use of prose. We cannot be certain that the whole text was written by Marlowe, but if we are looking at the overall style of the play, it is important to notice the effectiveness of the different methods of writing that are employed.

In the conversations between Wagner, the servants and the various country tradesmen, the down-to-earth, prosaic, coarse language is appropriate to the characters. The jokes, plays on words, tricks and deceits reflect their preoccupations with drink, women, lice and vermin. In Act I. Scene iv, when Wagner tries to persuade Robin to become his servant, he is promised a silken gown with plenty of 'stave-sacre' (a pest killer) to destroy any fleas lurking in the garment. The joking continues with stories about fleas. They are 'familiar' with the bodies on which they breed, but 'familiars' are also devilish attendants. Indeed two of the latter familiars are conjured up during the scene. This rough, punning comedy is continued throughout the servant scenes. In II.iii, Robin performs a crude travesty of Faustus's conjuration. He muddles up a few words and phrases that he has obviously overheard. His imagination so far is necromancy is concerned reaches no further

than obtaining wine without payment. He recites a mouthwatering list –
red wine, white wine, claret, sack, muscadine, malmsey, whippencrust
(all types of strong drink). In the characters of the horse courser and
the carter we hear the tediously detailed accounts of their unfortunate
dealings with Faustus. This gallery of country bumpkins, sharp and
slow-witted servants create in their speech and antics a vivid contrast
to the style of language and behaviour found in the more serious scenes.
This division, however, is not clear cut. In the episode in Rome we find
Faustus and Mephostophilis indulging in some fairly vigorous fooling,
with language to match. Whilst the basic style of blank verse remain,
variety is introduced with the heavy-handed rhyming couplets of
Mephostophilis's conjuration of the magic wand and girdle. The text
moves between verse and prose with the scene ending in a formal dirge
of excommunication interspersed by ludricrous denunciations of the
mysterious malefactors. We can see Marlowe adjusting his style of
writing to the requirements of the stage activity.

These various examples are sufficient to show the richness and
diversity of Marlowe's dramatic poetry in *Doctor Faustus*. We can
recognise the energetic strength of the blank verse, admire the flourish
and subtlety of his figurative language, enjoy the contrasting roughness
of the peasant speech; observing in all cases that the language is firmly
related to what is being performed on the stage. It is the careful,
imaginative combination of word and action that gives the play dramatic
vigour as well as poetic grandeur.

4.4 STAGECRAFT

The variety and richness of the language is matched by an equal diversity
in the stage presentation. The Prologue might lead us to expect a religious
drama in the pattern of a morality play. Certainly there are morality
figures such as the symbolic characters of the Good and Bad Angels
giving their contrary advice. The debates between Faustus and
Mephostophilis somewhat resemble a medieval disputation where the
participants occupy opposite chairs or pulpits and challenge each other
in formal question and answer. These exchanges together with the
soliloquies give a sense of highly disciplined drama where the emphasis
lies in the nature and quality of the argument rather than in any dramatic

effects. However if we look at the actual arrival of Mephostophilis we see that it is the first of a series of spectacular events that flood the stage with colour, excitement, exuberance and the weirdest creatures. The first shock is the appearance of Mephostophilis, far more frightening to Marlowe's audience than today's. An ugly, fearsome devil bursts upwards through the trapdoor in the stage. So horrible is this creature that Faustus immediately demands a change of identity and in the twinkling of an eye a soberly dressed friar replaces the scaly dragon. The dramatic arrival of this inhabitant of Hell as popularly depicted in wall paintings or statuary is in itself a spectacular piece of stagecraft, but the transmutation is equally skilful in refocusing our attention on to the serious business in hand. This appearance has firmly located Hell beneath the stage and it is into this inferno that Faustus will ultimately descend. With its establishment at the play's opening, we must feel uncomfortable when Faustus speaks of Hell so lightheartedly. But it is not only Mephostophilis that we meet. The Devil (Lucifer) himself appears along with his menacing cohorts. The scene in which Faustus draws the magic circle has Lucifer and four devils silently observing the conjuration, probably from a balcony above the main stage. This would be an unusual location for the devils, but perhaps their presence there reinforces Mephostophilis's grim reminder to Faustus: 'Why this is hell, nor am I out of it' (I.iv.75). A little later in the play Lucifer and Belzebub storm on to the stage and we see an actual close encounter with the Devil himself, not as a comic character but undoubtedly the Archregent of the Lower World. The devilish minions are also frightening, even when they are comic, because of the noise and explosions that seem always to accompany them. They are disconcertingly dangerous even when conjured by the servant Wagner.

Another form of surprise lies in the series of conjurations that follow the arrival of Mephostophilis. Devils entertain with a short dance as they offer a crown and rich garments to Faustus. A woman devil materialises as the proffered substitute for a wife. The spectacle increases in complexity with the Show of the Seven Deadly Sins. This is rather like a play within a play with Faustus as the favoured spectator allowed to converse with the performers. These characters, much in the style of morality play figures, vividly portray facets of sinful living, not by simple recitation, but by vigorous, individually characterised figures. There is no difficulty in picturing the ranting anger of self-wounding Wrath, the lazy, languorous complaining of Sloth or the insinuating sensuality of Lechery. All the characters are recognisably human in their selfish indulgence. The comedy is gross and vulgar. The shock is that this sensational, deeply unattractive display delights Faustus and succeeds, at least temporarily, in blotting from his mind thoughts of repentance.

The conjuration of the classic heroes takes a somewhat different form, resembling a dumb show (a device often used in Elizabethan and Jacobean plays). We are reminded that they are spirits and therefore untouchable. Yet the effect of the magic is to persuade the viewers that they are indeed in the presence of Alexander. The show is presented with such an eye to detail that even a mole on the neck of the paramour is included in the representation. The tone of this show is not comic, but induces wonder and astonishment as the figures move in stylised dramatic action accompanied by music and trumpet calls. Helen of Troy is also accompanied by the strains of music at her first appearance, and supported by two cupids on her second entry. The elegant, harmonious style belies the horror that lies below the surface of appearance.

Marlowe's inventive stagecraft is also demonstrated by the knock-about comedy in St Peter's, Rome. Here the jokes are physical and slapstick. Meat, a rare gift from the Bishop of Milan, is snatched from the Pope's mouth just as he is about to swallow it. Dainties from the Cardinal of France disappear just as rapidly, and so does the wine, and we have a hilarious scene of schoolboy japes with the most revered in church and state being made fools of. A clout on the ear finally decides the Pope to move on. The two pranksters disturb the dirge, beating the friars and chasing them with fireworks. To see Faustus and Mephostophilis indulging in this comic spectacle no doubt shocked and amused the audience. Such pranks and sleights of hand are also used to provide Benvolio with horns, the Duchess of Vanholt with grapes and to surprise the country traders with false heads and detachable legs.

The play offers a surprising mixture of tragically serious drama and the high jinks of low farce. This mixture has been criticised as a defect in the unity of the play, especially in the middle section, which certainly includes the greater proportion of the comic routines. But it is possible to see the deterioration of seriousness as an ironic comment on the foolish use that Faustus makes of his costly magic skills.

Records show that *Doctor Faustus* was performed by Philip Henslow's Company at the Rose Theatre on the south bank of the Thames, quite close to the famous Globe. This was a public theatre and the stage arrangement would certainly include a central trapdoor in the apron stage as well as a balcony. With provision for musicians and sound effects men in the upper storey, all the suggestions contained in the stagecraft discussion could have been readily carried out. The inventory of the stage properties used by the Company included 'i Hell mought'. Perhaps this was used in the Company's performance of *Doctor Faustus*.

5 SPECIMEN PASSAGE AND COMMENTARY

ACT I, SCENE iii

Thunder. Enter LUCIFER *and four devils (above).* FAUSTUS *to them with this speech.*

FAUSTUS: Now that the gloomy shadow of the night,
    Longing to view Orion's drizzling look,
    Leaps from th'antarctic world unto the sky,
    And dims the welkin with her pitchy breath,
    Faustus begin thine incantations
    And try if devils will obey thy hest,
    Seeing thou hast pray'd and sacrific'd to them.
    Within this circle is Jehovah's name
    Forward and backward anagrammatiz'd:
    Th'abbreviated names of holy saints,
    Figures of every adjunct to the heavens,
    And characters of signs and erring stars
    By which the spirits are enforc'd to rise.
    Then fear not, Faustus to be resolute
    And try the utmost magic can perform.   *[Thunder]*
    Sint mihi dei Acherontis propitii; valeat numen triplex
    Jehovae; ignei, aerii, acquatici, terreni spiritus salvete!
    Orientis princeps, Belzebub inferni ardentis monarcha, et
    Demogorgon, propitiamus vos, ut appareat, et surgat,
    Mephostophilis.   *Dragon.*
    Quid tu moraris? Per Jehovam, Gehennam, et consecratam

aquam quam nunc spargo, signumque crucis quod nunc facio, et
per vota nostra, ipse, nunc surgat nobis dicatus Mephostophilis.

Enter a Devil.

I charge thee to return and change thy shape,
Thou art too ugly to attend on me.
Go, and return an old Franciscan friar,
That holy shape becomes a devil best.   [*Exit Devil*]
I see there's virtue in my heavenly words.
Who would not be proficient in this art?
How pliant is this Mephostophilis,
Full of obedience and humility,
Such is the force of magic and my spells.
Now, Faustus, thou art conjuror laureate,
That canst command great Mephostophilis.
Quin redis Mephostophilis, fratris imagine?

Enter MEPHOSTOPHILIS.

MEPHOSTOPHILIS: Now, Faustus, what wouldst thou have me do?
FAUSTUS: I charge thee wait upon me whilst I live,
To do whatever Faustus shall command,
Be it to make the moon drop from her sphere,
Or the ocean to overwhelm the world.
MEPHOSTOPHILIS: I am a servant to great Lucifer,
And may not follow thee without his leave;
No more than he commands must we perform.
FAUSTUS: Did not he charge thee to appear to me?
MEPHOSTOPHILIS: No, I came now hither of mine own accord.
FAUSTUS: Did not my conjuring speeches raise thee? Speak.
MEPHOSTOPHILIS: That was the cause, but yet *per accidens*:
For when we hear one rack the name of God,
Abjure the scriptures and his saviour Christ,
We fly in hope to get his glorious soul:
Nor will we come unless he use such means
Whereby he is in danger to be damn'd.
Therefore the shortest cut for conjuring
Is stoutly to abjure the Trinity
And pray devoutly to the prince of hell.
FAUSTUS: So Faustus hath already done, and holds this principle:
There is no chief but only Belzebub,

To whom Faustus doth dedicate himself.
This word 'damnation' terrifies not him,
For he confounds hell in Elysium.
His ghost be with the old philosophers.
But leaving these vain trifles of men's souls,
Tell me, what is that Lucifer thy lord?

MEPHOSTOPHILIS: Arch-regent and commander of all spirits.

FAUSTUS: Was not that Lucifer an angel once?

MEPHOSTOPHILIS: Yes, Faustus, and most dearly lov'd of God.

FAUSTUS: How comes it then that he is prince of devils?

MEPHOSTOPHILIS: O, by aspiring pride and insolence,
For which God threw him from the face of heaven.

FAUSTUS: And what are you that live with Lucifer?

MEPHOSTOPHILIS: Unhappy spirits that fell with Lucifer,
Conspir'd against our God with Lucifer,
And are for ever damn'd with Lucifer.

FAUSTUS: Where are you damn'd?

MEPHOSTOPHILIS: In hell.

FAUSTUS: How comes it then that thou art out of hell?

MEPHOSTOPHILIS: Why, this is hell, nor am I out of it.
Think'st thou that I who saw the face of God
And tasted the eternal joys of heaven
Am not tormented with ten thousand hells
In being depriv'd of everlasting bliss?
O Faustus, leave these frivolous demands,
Which strike a terror to my fainting soul.

FAUSTUS: What, is great Mephostophilis so passionate
For being deprived of the joys of heaven?
Learn thou of Faustus, manly fortitude,
And scorn those joys thou never shalt possess.
Go, bear these tidings to great Lucifer:
Seeing Faustus hath incurr'd eternal death
By desperate thoughts against Jove's deity.
Say he surrenders up to him his soul,
So he will spare him four and twenty years,
Letting him live in all voluptuousness,
Having thee ever to attend on me,
To give me whatsoever I shall ask,
To tell me whatsoever I demand,

To slay mine enemies and aid my friends,
And always be obedient to my will.
Go, and return to mighty Lucifer,
And meet me in my study at midnight,
And then resolve me of thy master's mind.

MEPHOSTOPHILIS: I will, Faustus.

FAUSTUS: Had I as many souls as there be stars,
I'd give them all for Mephostophilis.
By him I'll be great emperor of the world,
And make a bridge thorough the moving air
To pass the ocean with a band of men;
I'll join the hills that bind the Afric shore,
And make that country continent to Spain,
And both contributory to my crown.
The Emperor shall not live but by my leave,
Nor any potentate of Germany.
Now that I have obtain'd what I desire
I'll live in speculation of this art
Till Mephostophilis return again.   [*Exit*]

[*Exeunt LUCIFER and DEVILS*]

COMMENTARY

This scene in which Faustus conjures the Devil falls into six sections.

1. Faustus begins the process of conjuration

The opening blank verse incantation begins with a series of dark images – 'gloomy shadows', 'drizzling look', 'pitchy breath' – that identify the midnight hour. It is suggested that night hurries up from the far south ('th'antarctic') and invades the northern world as daylight fades into pitch darkness. These phrases, accompanied by muttering thunder, create a sense of mysterious foreboding. Faustus forces the whole of the darkened world to focus on his act of conjuration. An abrupt command changes the tone and the diabolical invocation begins. Though the language speaks of 'Jehovah', 'holy saints', 'heavens', 'stars' and 'spirits', the words are being put to a devilish purpose. A mysterious chant consisting of complex polysyllabic sentences accompanies

Faustus's actions as he points out the marks and signs around the circumference of his magic circle. We heard of Jehovah's name 'forward and backward anagrammatiz'd' and of 'th'abbreviated names of holy saints'. These *names* are clearly being misused. God's name should not be meddled with in this way nor should the holy saints'. Faustus then braces himself for the actual conjuraton with the terse instruction, 'Then fear not, Faustus to be resolute'. The wide-ranging references and the mysterious incantation now converge on that terrifying moment when the Devil is called upon to manifest himself physically. Latin, the language of the church, is used for this unholy purpose in a travesty of religious observance. The Holy Trinity of God the Father, Son and Holy Ghost is replaced by the devilish trio of Lucifer, Belzebub and Demogorgon. Perhaps the audience would not fully understand the Latin, but words like 'Acherontis', 'Belzebub', 'inferni', 'monarcha', 'Demogorgon' would be sufficiently frightening. Marlowe skilfully holds back the Devil's arrival so that Faustus's words become more urgent and demanding. Will the invocation work? The first speech of Faustus sets the mood of dark mystery and grows in intensity to culminate in the great Latin recitation. The midnight hour, the thunder, the actual naming of the forces of evil create a sense of excited foreboding.

2. Appearance of the Devil

The spectacular appearance of the Devil on the stage is illustrated on the title page of the 1624 edition of the play and shows a fearsome, dragon-like monster bursting up through the floorboards while Faustus stands within the magic circle inscribed on the floor of his study. Despite this climactic appearance, Faustus is dissatisfied with the ugly shape of the devil. His commands are short, sharp and direct, emphasised by the alliteration of 'charge' and 'change' as well as the ironic suggestion that the 'holy shape' of a friar would best suit a 'devil'. Instantly, the devil obediently disappears. Now Faustus exults in his success. He is indeed 'conjuror laureate' and his 'heavenly' words have brought forth a 'pliant' Mephostophilis, 'full of obedience and humility'. Now the irony becomes inescapable. The success in which Faustus delights is to be anything but heavenly and he will soon discover the very severe limits to Mephostophilis's obedience and humility. Nevertheless the whole tone of the scene has now changed from sombre expectancy to delighted exultation. Terse phrases of command are juxtaposed with longer, more complexly phrased thoughts of conjuration and power.

3. Reappearance of Mephostophilis

Now we actually hear the Devil's agent speak. The exchanges are direct and matter-of-fact so far as Mephostophilis is concerned, but Faustus's demands mount to hyperbolic proportions – 'to make the moon drop from her sphere', 'the ocean to overwhelm the world'. When we hear the explanations for the appearance of Mephostophilis we begin to sense the imperfect nature of Faustus's control. When a human being is heard to 'rack the name of God' or 'abjure the Scriptures', 'abjure the Trinity' and then pray devoutly to the devil – all totally irreligious acts – then is his 'glorious' soul greatly imperilled. Whilst Mephostophilis's words intensify the religious dimension with his references to God, Christ and the Trinity, Faustus emphasises the infernal world with talk of Belzebub, the futility of damnation and old-fashioned theories of Hell which are dismissed as 'vain trifles'. Mephostophilis makes abundantly clear the path to damnation. Ironically, Faustus foolishly disregards the implications of his actions.

4. Discussion of Hell and the identity of Lucifer

Faustus persists in his disregard, even in the discussion that follows when Mephostophilis tells the story of the Fall of Lucifer, stressing their earlier existences as angels in heaven, terminated by that same aspiring pride that Faustus is, at that moment, demonstrating. More ironic still is Mephostophilis's urgent appeal to Faustus to put aside 'these frivolous demands'. His speech contrasting the 'eternal joys of heaven' with the deprivation of 'everlasting bliss' makes no impact on the self-confident Faustus. Rejection of such forceful advice is both ironic and terrifying. How can he ignore such forthright, first-hand evidence?

5. Faustus proposes the details of the contract

'Manly fortitude' is sufficient defence declares Faustus as he sets out the terms of his proposed contract. He will surrender his soul for twenty-four years of voluptuousness and the services of Mephostophilis who defers to these demands 'to give', 'to tell', 'to slay', to 'be obedient' with a simple 'I will'. His expostulations have been fruitless and Faustus's words express disdainful incomprehension of what is implied in his demands. His tone to Mephostophilis is mocking and arrogant. He does not perceive the foolish imbalance of his proposed bargain with Lucifer. He knows he will be deprived of 'the joys of heaven' as was Mephostophilis, he knows he has 'incurr'd eternal death' but that knowledge makes no effect on his decision.

6. Faustus considers the use of his new-found power

Now he begins a great reverie as he dreams of all the wonders that he will perform. The scene concludes with an example of Marlowe at his most expansive, grand and universal. Faustus's mind moves over continents – Africa, Spain, Germany. He will build a great bridge across the oceans strong enough to carry a whole army of men. Africa will be joined to Spain. He will become pre-eminent with every emperor and potentate at his command. We listen to this breathtaking, imaginative excursion with amazement. The scene ends, as it began, with 'world' images.

*   *   *

The speeches show Marlowe's firm, imaginative control of the blank verse form. The intensity and feeling is enhanced rather than restricted by the regular beat of the iambic pentameters. The rhythm adds weight to the incantation. The meaning often runs over more than one line so that the structure is flowing and continuous. Ideas are joined by the regular use of 'and' (parataxis). There is a frequent shift of style through soliloquy, formal invocation, direct conversation and elaborate reverie. A vivid, poignant portrait is painted of Lucifer (strengthened by the constant repetition of his name). The joys of Heaven are contrasted with the torment, deprivation and terrors of Hell. The irony contained in these comparisons is lost on Faustus but is only too obvious to the listener.

Staging

The visual effects in this scene are very spectacular. The stage directions indicate that above Faustus, and unseen by him throughout the scene, is Lucifer with attendant devils. The conjuration results in the appearance of a frightful monster through the trapdoor. The audience would be shocked, perhaps frightened by this horrible apparition appearing before them but the creature is quickly dismissed to reappear in the guise of a Christian monk. Marlowe uses the popular tradition associated with the appearance of the Devil with smoke, thunder and explosions but he quickly switches back to a more subtle dramatic image by cloaking the devil in the habit of a Franciscan friar. We should note that this scene is followed immediately by the comic conjuration of the servant Wagner who uses his magic skill to impress a foolish country boy. In the event, Faustus does little more in his conjuration than does his servant. The difference is that Wagner has not forfeited his soul.

6 CRITICAL RECEPTION

6.1 INTRODUCTION

Records in sixteenth- and seventeenth-century diaires, journals and
theatre accounts show evidence of the great popularity of *Doctor
Faustus* in the theatre. As well as being performed in London, the play
toured England and Europe, and proved to be exciting both for audience
and actors. A report of one early performance in Exeter described a
rather frightening experience.

> Certaine Players at Exeter, acting upon the stage the tragical storie
> of Dr. Faustus the Conjuer; as a certain number of Devels kept everie
> one his circle there, and as Faustus was busie in his magicall invoca-
> tions, on a sudden they were all dasht, every one harkning other in
> the eare, for they were all perswaded, there was one devell too many
> amongst them; and so after a little pause desired the people to
> pardon them, they could go no further with this matter; the people
> also understanding the thing as it was, every man hastened to be
> first out of dores. The players (as I heard it) contrarye to their
> custom spending the night in reading and in prayer got them out of
> the town the next morning.
>
> (printed in D. J. Palmer, 'Magic and Poetry in *Doctor Faustus*')

On this occasion, the conjuration was more than usually successful and
Lucifer himself seemed to have provided one of the devils.

Contemporary written criticism of Marlowe emphasised his atheism and blasphemies. Thomas Beard in his book *Theatre of God's Judgments* published in 1597 wrote of Marlin (Marlowe):

> Not inferior to any of the former in Atheisme and impietie, and equall to all in maner of punishment, was one of our own nation, of fresh and late memorie, called Marlin [Marlowe], by profession a scholler, brought up from his youth in the Universitie of Cambridge, but by practise a Play-maker, and a Poet of scurrilitie, who by giving too large a swinge to his own wit, and suffering his lust to have the full reines, fell (not without just desert) to that outrage and extremitie, that he denied God and his sonne Christ, and not only in word blasphemed the Trinitie, but also (as it is credibly reported) wrote bookes against it, affirming our Saviour to be but a deceiver, and Moses to be but a conjurer and seducer of the people, and the holy Bible to be vaine and idle stories, and all religion but a device of policie.

> (in Judith O'Neill (ed.), *Critics on Marlowe*)

It was Marlowe's fellow playwrights and poets who showed most approval of his skills as a poet and dramatist. Samuel Pepys recorded in his diary in 1662 that he took his wife to see a production of *Doctor Faustus* and left profoundly unimpressed by the poor performance.

6.2 THE PLAY IN PERFORMANCE

We have to move to the twentieth century to find regular revivals of the play. Three productions during the last ten years have demonstrated the vigorous appeal of the play as well as illuminating the severe problems posed by the uncertainties surrounding the text. The play received widely differing dramatic treatment in terms of characterisation and presentation – all providing fuel to the critics voicing their approval or disapproval. A production in 1974 by the Royal Shakespeare Company with Ian McKellen in the title role was directed by a noted Shakespeare scholar, John Barton. In a programme note he described the way the text for the performance had been put together.

Weighty critical opinion holds that Marlowe himself wrote only about 39% of the play, and the rest is by an unknown author. . . . I have selected from and combined the 'A' and 'B' versions so that the production includes over 1100 lines from one or other of these two texts, of which just under 800 are probably by Marlowe . . . I have, for example, removed all but one of the sub-plot scenes. Though in theory the sub-plots provide a complementary comment on the main action by showing the abuse of necromantic powers in trivial pranks, in practice they tend to trivialise the tone of the play itself. At least, that has been the experience of myself and many others on seeing the play in the theatre. Also, bearing in mind that the bulk of the scenes most certainly written by Marlowe are set in Faustus's study, I decided to present the whole play as taking place there. To achieve this I have had to change the location of three scenes. . .and to omit the other (the Pope scene) which could not be played there.

My excisions have been counter-balanced by the addition of about 550 lines, mostly deriving from Marlowe's source, *The History of the Damnable Life of Dr. Faustus*, commonly known as the English *Faust-Book*.

(John Barton, Programme Note *Doctor Faustus*, Royal Shakespeare Theatre, September, 1974)

Such a director's note should be sufficient to warn readers that any performances of *Doctor Faustus* they may see will not necessarily resemble the printed text that they have studied. Here we find a combination of the two texts with material from the non-dramatic *Faus-Book*. In performance, the audience found even more startling modifications. The Seven Deadly Sins, Helen of Troy and the Good and Bad Angels were represented by puppets. This reduction in scale changed the impact of the Shows and supernatural interventions. By placing the action in Faustus's study – a room full of alcoves, over-stuffed with furniture, books, atlases, maps, globes, pipes, writing materials – the suggestion was made that the spectacles and conjurations were manifestations of what was happening in Faustus's mind. A dark-robed, sombre-toned Mephostophilis (Emrys James), his forehead marked with a black spot, lurked always in the background. With the removal of the comic scenes, the play became a carefully patterned, intellectual exploration of the protagonist's dilemma rather than a spectacular epic that swept Faustus towards destruction.

A production directed by Christopher Fettes, presented at the Lyric, Hammersmith in 1980 took a somewhat different approach, including many of the comic scenes that John Barton had omitted, and restoring a good deal of the 1616 text. Most of the small cast of eight doubled several parts, for instance Simon Cutler played the Bad Angel, Robin, Lechery and Helen of Troy, whilst the diminutive David Rappaport was ironically cast as both Belzebub and Pope, as well as being Dick and Adrian. The play was set around a long, heavy library table, piled with books where Faustus (James Aubrey) was found at work among gowned students, angled so that their faces were scarcely visible. Among these anonymous figures and undistinguished from them were the Good and Bad Angels – the latter marked only by a black gloved hand – and a fierce, magnetic, yet world-weary Mephostophilis (Patrick Magee) manipulating the books as Faustus perused them. There was no escaping the close physical presence of these advisers. In the Rome scenes, the table became an elevated platform for the Pope's throne (ascended via the bowed back of the captive, chained Bruno). Stretched out on that same table, Faustus experienced his death agonies as the devils tore at him.

The tableaux were presented in transparently curtained booths placed at the rear of the stage. Careful lighting and stylised movement lent horror to the deadly sins, majestic power to Alexander and intense attractiveness to Helen whom Faustus clasped in a loving embrace.

The simplified staging and the stylised acting gave a unity to the production despite the diversity of scenes and the changes between tragedy and comedy. A critic wrote: 'The main virtue from which all other stem, is that the text itself is vividly present throughout – always audible, and even at its more obscure never slurred over.' (James Fenton, *The Sunday Times*, 2 March 1980). A programme note associated Faustus's longing for greater power with the Greek word *pothos*.

The greatest exemplary of *pothos* in antiquity was Alexander the Great. He is said to have himself invented the phrase 'seized by pothos' to account for his indescribable longing for something beyond, a longing that carried him beyond all borders in a horizontal conquest of space, a true 'space man' of ancient times. . . Space and distance became the visual image that released his yearning.

(James Hillman, *Loose Ends* in Programme Note, Lyric Studio, 1980)

The production, though much criticised, acquired an integrity by virtue of the director's respect for the text and his realisation of the central theme of 'intense longing' in a sensitive, stylised production.

In March, 1984 The Marlowe Society at Cambridge presented *Doctor Faustus* as its annual production. The director, David Parry, came to his task with a great experience of medieval drama production. His approach to the play was:

> through the earlier traditions of popular theatre still very much alive in Marlowe's youth - the great Mystery Cycles and the morality plays with their vivid imagery of the forces of Heaven and Hell, their directness of approach to the audience, their wonderful mixture of high seriousness and rough humour, and their sense that every aspect of the visible world reflects the meaning and nature of the invisible, the supernatural, the divine. Marlowe's aspirations may be those of the Renaissance; he may use medieval images and traditions only to twist and shatter them. But his play stands poised between the old world and the new, and our recognition of the traditions from which it comes.
>
> (D. Parry, Programme Note *Doctor Faustus*, Marlowe Society, Cambridge, 1984)

The staging, though modern, reflected many of the characteristics of the Elizabethan stage with an upper gallery from which Lucifer or his minions were constantly on watch, and an open apron stage with trapdoors affording access from below. Entrances were provided at the rear of the stage allowing access for the dumb shows and spectacles. The production was accompanied by the necessary fireworks, smoke, thunder and music. The vigorous playing of the comic scenes was continued when Faustus jubilantly joined in the fun. There was a small cast with a duplication of parts made effective by the use of masks for the Angels and spirits. A strong feeling of irony pervaded this production as one watched the frivolous use that Faustus made of his necromantic skills, highlighted particularly in the comic conjuring scenes. The text used on this occasion was a composite version of the A and B texts.

A programme note by Ann Barton in the Royal Shakespeare Company production referred to earlier commented:

In putting the play on the stage, a director must decide what to keep and what to exclude, how to weld the best of both versions into a single, acting text that is as close as possible to the lost, authoritative manuscript. He can never be sure that he is right. He faces interpretative problems, also, of equal complexity. *Doctor Faustus* is a play which looks in contrary directions simultaneously. It can be regarded as . . . a testament of belated orthodoxy, a sombre acquiescence to Christianity on the part of a dramatist whose atheism, spectacular though it seemed, was at bottom nervous and unsure. It can also be seen as the central document of Renaissance free-thinking: the tragedy of a man who, for all his faults, nonetheless nourishes a marvellous dream of scientific and humane power which the universe is too niggardly to allow. In the world of *Doctor Faustus*, nothing is simple or clear-cut. The play follows a didactic, morality play pattern – the story of Everyman tempted, sinning, unable to repent, and damned – but it questions or contradicts this orthodoxy at every turn.

These three contrasting productions illustrate and illuminate analysis of the play. The first emphasised the introspective Faustus with the battle essentially in his mind. The second, in which Faustus remained a young man throughout the play offered a 'drama derived from interaction between passionate adolescent minds and powerful books' (James Fenton, *The Sunday Times*) and a 'fascination for magic' (Robert Zarkin, *Plays & Players*, May 1980). The third interpretation acted as a reminder of a strong dramatic heritage in religious drama with Faustus at the centre of a crowded earth with vigilant supernatural beings ready to pounce and destroy when opportunity offered. No production utilised all the text of either version, but selected, combined or amended the script and in one case added new material.

6.3 LITERARY CRITICISM

When we turn to literary criticism of the play, we find quite different attitudes and emphases being explored. We have already noted the far from settled arguments about the validity of the texts, but the critics' and commentators' main preoccupations are in interpreting the themes of the play, quite separately from any concern with performance.

In the first part of *Critics on Marlowe*, Judith O'Neill has usefully summarised a selection of critical views of the play given between the sixteenth and twentieth centuries. In none is there a mention of performance but rather a response to Marlowe's unusual imagination. Hazlitt commented on 'a hunger and thirst after unrighteousness, a glow of the imagination, unhallowed by anything but its own energies'. Swinburne wrote: 'he gave wings to English poetry'. A more recent critic, Una Ellis Fermor believed 'in that deeper, inner world where not men's differences but their common and essential likeness is in question, he moves, as a master'.

In 'Marlowe's Faustus: A Reconsideration', in *The Review of English Studies*, vol. XIX, (1943), Leo Kirschbaum began to talk about the play in terms of its effects in the theatre and the need temporarily to respond to, but not ultimately accept, its values. These, he claimed, were undoubtedly Christian, and must be acknowledged if the play were to have validity as drama. But that very positive assertion did not prevent further extensive and detailed interpretations proposing often quite contrary viewpoints. They were, of course, hinted at in Ann Barton's programme note.

Harry Levin's *The Overreacher* (Faber & Faber, 1954) included the following passage:

> Where the *Mirror for Magistrates* darkly reflected the falls of princes, Marlowe exhibits the rise of commoners. His heroes make their fortunes by exercising virtues which conventional morality might well regard as vices. For the most part, they are self-made men; and to the extent that they can disregard the canons of good and evil, they are supermen. All of Marlowe's plays are dominated . . . by the conflicts between virtue and fortune. . .between the energies of the protagonist and the circumstances into which he hurls himself. As it is repeated, the pattern is varied and elaborated; the characterization, starting with the crudest and broadest strokes, increasingly registers subtlety and depth. (p.48)

This overall interpretation of Marlowe's heroes does seem to provide a useful basis to interpret *Doctor Faustus* The chapter on the particular play is entitled 'Science without Conscience' and demonstrates the hazards of scientific overreaching regardless of the consequences. The religious references are acknowledged but not seen to be at the centre of the tragedy. We are engaged by 'the energies' of Faustus and 'the circumstances into which he hurls himself'.

Commentators who refer to the tragedy's connections with the morality play stress the formal pattern of those dramas - a fall followed by redemption which later, under Protestant theology, became a fall followed by damnation. *Doctor Faustus* comes into this later category, but as J. P. Brockbank noted in *Marlowe: Dr. Faustus*: *Perspectives of Criticism*, (1962) '*Dr. Faustus*. . . retains the great rival simplicities; from the one side a continuing reverence for the moral processes of God's justice; and from the other, a continuing delight in knowledge of the created world.' (p.21)

All the morality plays, however, emphasised that concluding final judgement and Marlowe undoubtedly uses specifically Christian images in the final scene. The tortured man sees Christ's streaming blood - symbolising the mercy that he has rejected - and then faces the fierce God of Judgement. The devils do emerge from a physical Hell and claim Faustus's soul. The evidence of Christian judgement and condemnation is inescapably present.

The modern reader might not, like Faustus, be 'terrified' by damnation, but prefers to admire the brave audacity of the man who is willing to experiment in the Black Arts, as today we hear of experimentation with hallucinating drugs. In this case Marlowe presents what Irving Ribner calls a 'Promethean Faustus'. In an article comparing Macbeth with Marlowe's hero he writes:

In *Dr. Faustus* there is no real alternative to the damnation [he] must suffer. For him to have accepted the offer of mercy which is constantly extended to him by the Good Angel and urged by the Old Man, and against the temptation of which he struggles throughout the play would have been to deny those very aspirations to rise beyond the state of ignorant and impotent man which had led him to pledge his soul to Lucifer, and which have lent him the heroic stature which renders him a tragic figure. It is, after all, the Promethean Faustus who will not accept the limitations of humanity who captivates our imagination and prevents us from seeing this play as a simple Christian morality play teaching the fate of the unrepentant sinner.

('Marlowe's "Tragicke Glasse"' in R. Hosley (ed.) *Essays of Shakespeare and Elizabethan Drama in Honor of Hardin Craig* (Columbia: Mass., 1962))

The varied interpretations placed on the play by directors and critics reveal the rich, subtle complexity of Marlowe's drama. A significant difference has become obvious when we compare the productions and the literary commentaries. We have also learnt the sharp difference between the 'dramatic text', that which is written: and the 'performance text', the words spoken by the actors on the stage. The director is forced by the demands of performance to commit himself to an interpretation of the play that will work in the theatre, whilst the critic is under no such constraint and is free to conjecture at will with no obligation to settle firmly for one or other of the theories, nor to test their views in practical terms.

Broadly speaking the choices open to us are as follows:

1. The play as a whole is concerned with the damnation of a scholar who challenges the established cosmic order and suffers as a consequence.
2. We may see the play in moral (but not specifically religious) terms where the hero willingly hazards all for the chance of rich rewards and supreme authority, and fails.
3. Faustus is a rebel, asserting the primacy of man against all other forces, a risk taker, one who celebrates life in vigorous action, including comic excursions, but tragically finds that his experiments in these new fields collapse about him. We admire his energetic pursuit of fresh knowledge and feel saddened by his failure.

A religious reading of the play utilises well-recognised theological conceptions such as presumption (Lucifer was the first example), damnation, the just punishment of the unrepentant and the sin of despair which represents a denial of God's forgiving mercy that must inevitably lead to condemnation.

The term 'Renaissance man' is aptly applied to Faustus the challenger, the explorer of forbidden territories, ready to take risks involving hostility, danger and destruction because of his powerful assertion that man has the life, the intelligence and the right to mastery of the universe.

There can be no doubt that contrary feelings, emotions and desires fight for supremacy in Faustus's mind. This battle may be symbolised on the stage by small puppets, human figures or grotesquely masked supernatural spirits. The first concept makes for a play of introspection, brooding over weighty decisions, seldom moving from Faustus's study. Alternatively those mental pressures might be identified by human characters, at first unrecognised, yet who press their advice (good or bad) on a man beset with a great unfulfilled longing for power. But if the world is a stage with Heaven and Hell having distinct and real existences, then Faustus as a distinguished theological scholar and man of the world will struggle with his conscience in a series of confrontations, arguments, tricks and deceits that show his mind and emotions working as they react to each new situation. Contemplation is replaced by argument, reverie by action, disdain for authority by trickery, and damnation by physical disintegration.

Readers must weigh the evidence and reach their own conclusions. The marvel is that a play written four hundred years ago can bear such investigation and invite such contemporary interpretation that Faustus's dilemma remains a reality for us in the sophisticated twentieth century.

John Faustus is not an archaic figure. We see in his struggles and failures dilemmas which still present themselves today even though they are not expressed in terms of magical conjurations or threats of damnation. The modern overreacher is tempted with political power and military might backed by an arsenal of Satanic weapons capable of causing total annihilation. The forces for good, like the Good Angel and the Old Man seem impotent to prevent the threats of destruction, yet a desire for 'salvation' in terms of peace and freedom still struggles with desperate urgency to make itself heard. We might phrase the words of the Epilogue differently, but the warning remains: 'Power is seductively attractive: be wary of its use.'

REVISION QUESTIONS

1. Compare the portraits of Faustus that are presented (a) at the beginning of the play, (b) at the end of Act IV, and (c) at the close of Act V. What are the important changes in his character and attitudes?

2. How effectively is (a) good, and (b) evil portrayed in the play? Compare and contrast their stage representatives.

3. T. S. Eliot wrote of Marlowe's 'savage, comic humour'. What examples could you supply from *Doctor Faustus*?

4. Select and comment on scenes that, in your opinion, demonstrate (a) Marlowe's poetic gifts, (b) his ability to dramatise discussion, and (c) his skill in stagecraft.

5. Dramatic conflict is said to be an essential ingredient of tragedy. How is this conflict developed and sustained in *Doctor Faustus*?

6. 'How greatly is it all planned' (Goethe). Comment on this view of the dramatic structure of *Doctor Faustus*.

7. Can Faustus be truly regarded as a tragic hero?

8. How successful is Marlowe in combining the human and supernatural elements in *Doctor Faustus*? Illustrate your answer with specific examples.

9. Do the comic scenes represent a debasement of an otherwise serious tragic drama?

FURTHER READING

Texts

Greg, W.W. (ed.), *Marlowe's Dr. Faustus 1604–1616: Parallel Texts* (Clarendon Press, 1950).

Jump, John D. (ed.), *Dr. Faustus* (Methuen, 1962).

Gill, Roma (ed.), *Dr. Faustus* (Benn, 1967).

Pendry, E.D. and Maxwell, J.C. (eds), *Christopher Marlowe: Complete Plays and Poems* (Dent, 1976).

Commentaries

Brockbank, J.P., *Marlowe: Dr. Faustus* (Arnold, 1962).

Campbell, Lily, 'Dr. Faustus: A Case of Conscience' in *P.M.L.A.*, vol. LXVII (1952).

Cole, Douglas, *Suffering and Evil in the Plays of Christopher Marlowe* (Princeton, 1962).

Farnham, W. (ed.), *Twentieth-Century Interpretations of 'Dr. Faustus'* (Prentice-Hall, 1969).

Hotson, J. Leslie, *The Death of Christopher Marlowe* (London, 1925).

Jump, John (ed.), *Marlowe: Dr. Faustus* (Macmillan, 1969).

Leech, Clifford (ed.), *Marlowe: A Collection of Critical Essays* (New Jersey, 1964).

Levin, H., *The Overreacher* (Faber & Faber, 1954).

Maxwell, J.C., 'The Plays of Christopher Marlowe' in B. Ford (ed.), *Guide to English Literature: Age of Shakespeare*, vol. 2 (Penguin, 1961).

O'Neill, Judith (ed.), *Critics on Marlowe* (Allen & Unwin, 1969).

Palmer, D.J., 'Magic and Poetry in *Doctor Faustus*' in Jump, J. (ed.), *Marlowe: Doctor Faustus* (Macmillan, 1969).

Salgado, Gamini, 'Christopher Marlowe', in C. Ricks (ed.), *Sphere History of Literature*, vol. 3 (Sphere), 1971).

Sanders, Wilbur, *The Dramatist and the Received Idea* (Cambridge University Press, 1968).

Steane, J.B., *Marlowe: A Critical Study* (Cambridge University Press, 1965).

Wilson, F.P., *Marlowe and Early Shakespeare* (Oxford University Press, 1953).